CLOCKW
ORK OF
SUBJECT
IVITY

Contents

"Any sense in which life fails to resolve itself so too for death, only more so."

—Depth For Its Own Sake

BOOK 1: ETHOS ANTHROPOS DAIMON

Part 1: Spirit.

1.

Marx's error.—Philosophy does not change the world, philosophy discovers the ways the world is already changing. Philosophy does not 'create', it discovers; as when philosophy creates a new concept it has discovered for the first time a way that the world already is, and is changing. To emphasize creating over discovering is to deny and depower philosophy. The myth of God is that he created out of nothing; this is really symbolic of the self-creating process of deep discovery.

2.

Weaknesses are errors only when they fail to be paired with strengths. And when paired with strengths: the cultivation and edification of personality.

3.

Desire has its own rationality, and any will to truth that fails to account for desire does not deserve to be called reasonable.

4.

What is the deepest concept in philosophy? It is the concept of thought itself, which links closely with fantasy; thought lives through the fantasy- image and is grounded in it, springs from it like pliant soft   reeds from moist soil, while the fantasy-image uses thought to objectify itself into the world in order that it may make itself available to our desire. Desires are the shadows of our fantasies, for every desire seeks to complete the circle of image to thought to action and back again to image. From where then do fantasies come, and why? What is the truth of our fantasizing, and what is its power? It must be distinguished that power which fantasy is and expresses from that power from which fantasy comes. The raison d'être of desire is fantasy-completion, while the raison d'être of thought is the enabling and furthering of desires; so what is the raison d'être of fantasy itself, of the fantasy-image? Philosophy has not yet seriously asked this question, perhaps because the answer is merely "that which oneself is". Self-valuing[1] is the logic that holds a self together, and its first order principle of valuing is manifested as the whole varied host of the images of fantasy. Those images are the "glue" that holds a self together.

5.

Phenomenology as poison.—'Meaning' is a poison on the fantasy-image; a warped reality-principle.

6.

The secret purpose of poetry.—We must mystify the depths of our hearts, in order to keep these depths from becoming exhausted in articulation.

7.

Dare we also say, therefore, that so much of philosophy has been merely and secretly... poetry?

---

[1] Jakob Milikowski as credited with the notion of self- valuing.

8.

The most fundamental conceptual opposition in philosophy, and therefore the most fundamental conceptual opposition as such, is that of truth to power, and power to truth. While fantasy may be the fundamental philosophical human concept, a psychological 'gestalt' that may never be reduced to the "quantum foam" of all the history and value of man and his quite accidental experiences and leanings out of which such a fantasy has emerged, quite chaotically and irreducibly, it is the case that at the level of the mind, of proper thought and of philosophy it is truth and power that govern the world. Truth may reduce itself to power and power may reduce itself to truth, but neither of these reductions may reduce itself to the other reduction. Nietzsche's interpretation of the will to truth as will to power is therefore a partial reduction of truth to power, but this tells only one half of the story; what about the reduction of the will to power to will to truth? What of the reduction of power itself to truth? Such an operation cannot take place or be framed within the context of the will to power as such, for power and truth are both empty concepts 'in themselves'. Philosophy proceeds according to three movements, each of which has been attempted only partially so far: the movement of truth to power, the movement of power to truth, and the movement of both truth and power to the fantasy- image. Philosophy has invented many beautiful concepts for these partial movements—hope, love, desire, conquest; also truth, and power, and... philosophy.

9.

Simplicity of consciousness.—Consciousness is having perspective, and having perspective is having contents in mentality and as mentality; those innumerable contents (our memories, our sensations) are then organized logically so as to produce a perspective—on themselves. These early perspectives then subsequently enter into the sea of mental contents from which they are derived and become new, meta-contents (such as our ideas, speech, and a sense of oneself as a discrete and consistent entity). Eventually these meta contents are also logically organized so as to produce a super-perspective, and this subsequent and derivative organizing of the meta contents is what is called philosophy, which gives rise to a higher perspective, to a consciousness of consciousness. Here enters will and intentionality, also what is called morality, and also not merely a sense of self but a self as substance.

10.

Lowly (which is to say common) moralities cloud a more certain and clear judgment—this is not a side effect of such moralities but rather their primary purpose.

11.

Personality is a mask that comes to life, so that we may come to wear more interesting masks.

12.

Politics.—Reason is currently being split in two, so that the underlying subjective psychological excess may eventually be freed from its current entrapment in mere dialectics.

13.

Strength, like justice, serves as its own reward.

14.

The difference between strength and savagery is often found later, in the results.

15.

Man struggles to overcome death because he does not know how to struggle to overcome life.

16.

Ethos of philosophy.—Men are either gods, or—men.

17.

Every action in this world, from that of the lowliest worm to that of the highest human genius, is the projection of a value.

18.

Power must be interpreted through the lens of truth, and truth must be interpreted through the lens of power. And then these two interpretations must be interpreted through each other. This is the road to the future philosophy.

19.

Clockwork of subjectivity 1.—What is the nature of the fantasy-image? The fantasy-image is the promise of hope itself, the promise of achievement of every desire and the termination of every need and longing in perfect satiation. In so far as men are always "psychological" the power of the fantasy-image cannot be denied. Even when this power has been suppressed and hidden away in shame or impotence, it nonetheless manifests itself all the more complexly and subtly as a result—not only as the driving force of behavior and the governing logic organizing our instincts into a resonant whole, but also as the underlying "unconscious" force behind mentality itself, behind thought. Thought cannot escape the fantasy-image and its fundamental influence over mentality, for thought is a value- reflection of the two primary principles of truth and power, and truth and power ultimately converge and bury themselves in the fantasy-image, and to this fact it is irrelevant whether or not the fantasy-image in a particular mentality expresses itself more as form or as content. For while content may be suppressed and resisted, often on account of a common and petty moralism, or simply out of personal impotent weakness before oneself and others, this suppression of the contents of the fantasy-image simply converts the fantasy-image into a more formal structure, something a bit more hollowed- out and "unconscious". This is the "psychological complexity and ressentimental depth" that Nietzsche observed was greater in the slave morality than in the master morality. Man cannot escape his fantasy-image, for it is bound to him irrevocably, and he to it, in so far as there is no distinction between "him" and the image that rules him. It is thus apparent how the mutual slave and master relationship (a much higher-order master/slave relationship than the one Nietzsche identified) that exists between man and his fantasy-image, in which both man and the image take part and take turns in playing both the master and the slave, is the true source of human freedom.

20.

Clockwork of subjectivity 2.—The world is nothing but the conditions for man's fulfilling of the fantasy-image. This is the true meaning of the Garden of Eden, that man took over from God the responsibility of reality-creation—by taking possession of the two greatest key-sets, those of power and of truth—when man discovered his fantasy-image; or perhaps when the fantasy-image and man both discovered each other. This is also the deeper meaning of love and of all "objectification".

21.

Clockwork of subjectivity 3.—Love is when two people objectify each other in sufficient measure such that each objectification ensures the value of the respective fantasy-images. Truth and power are thereby tied into and through each other, forming a resonant bond on which the production of a new world may begin. We objectify precisely what we are already able to love through our own mastery, and we love what has already served us in being objectified.

22.

I will say but one thing regarding the state of modern 'philosophy', for the subject does not deserve mention from our sacred lips; nonetheless perhaps a single observation is warranted: Modern philosophy has asserted its power at the expense of truth, and is thereby losing that power. Modern philosophy housed in academia has made the declaration that philosophers may only operate or have influence within the academic sphere, by submitting to its supposed power and authority; by memorizing countless reams of published papers, irrelevant historical minutia, and by turning oneself into a repository of the personalities of others by slavishly adhering to all the absurd arcana and sub-micro-specialized terminologies and silly arguments that the student is forced to expend himself confronting. What utter uselessness, what nonsense is modern philosophy. The control of publication and degree granting that masks for the prestige of philosophy is a low point in the history of philosophy, and it is no wonder that so few truly great minds emerge from such a barren soil. Modern philosophy would be ashamed of itself, were it honest and earthy enough to feel shame; since it is not it merely proceeds in its dirge

11

toward nothingness. This failure of academia has arisen due to it having been taken over by lowly minds, by losers who do not know how to respect and admire their betters. We true philosophers could declare war on academic philosophy, but since when do men declare war on ants? The machinery of the world is already moving to crush this infestation of modern philosophy, indeed this infestation presages its own destruction at its own hands. An apology to ants: even ants are of an infinitely higher order of being than are these modern "philosophers".

23.

Clockwork of subjectivity 4.—Empathy is a superficial structure and not a fundamental of consciousness. We do not care about others because we empathize with them, we empathize with others because we care about them (to the degree that we really do care about them, for reasons having nothing to do with our empathy.)

24.

Clockwork of subjectivity 5.—Following beauty is indistinguishable from following the moral good, in so far as "moral good" really means that which it means: truth itself, truth blazing a path through the ontology of the world and discovering that core element which manifests itself in each of us as a fundamental purpose and pleasure, an euphoric-erotic raison d'être. Beauty is the life of the fantasy-image, guarded by the vast powers of what is called emotion, also what is called meaning, although any meaning taken outside of this context becomes poisonous and dark, like a spirit in the body that has decided to try and defeat its host. The true source of evil is always the same in all cases where evil appears: the vampiric draining of meaning from the core fundament of the fantasy-image, the misalignment of the machinery of conscience such that those experiences which are not properly meaningful in a more vital and true context are mistaken to be vitally meaningful in themselves, so that a separate core is established in subjectivity and dissonance follows. This dissonance obscures the self to itself by preventing its higher-order self-valuing integration; thus does the self fragment into its constituent parts which then seek war upon one another, for they have lost their cohesion in being formative of a self with regard to exercising the principles of truth and power. Truth without power is naïveté, but power without truth is mere banality. Dissonance thus forms a will to power, to power alone and for its own sake, and for the sake of forcing the disjointed aspects of the self into submission through conquest and through the abruption of the grounding-birthing logic of the fantasy-image with regard to how the fantasy image is that which wields the dual meta-psychic flows of truth-to-power and power-to-truth. Beauty cannot survive in this dissonance, for beauty is the child of the grounding-birthing logic at root in the tectonic depths of the intersubjective existentia. Beauty stands in for the capacity and might of the fantasy-image to deny power when that power comes at the expense of truth; the more savage and narcissistic, vain intellect and unbreakable bond of supremely confident will and certainty of self is the opposite of beauty in this regard, namely stands in for the capacity and might of the fantasy-image to deny truth when that truth comes at the expense of power. Thus beauty and "self-confidence" form a highly derivative, meta-logical daemonic polarity whose tension acts as a guiding compass and divining rod for the self. "Morality" is nothing but a beautiful concept we have given to recognize our self- responsibility, but this must be paired with self- confidence in order for our responsibility to remain naturally centered in the tripartite axis where truth, power and the fantasy-image meet.

25.

Clockwork of subjectivity 6.—The beginning part of pleasure is attraction and desire, which is an experience of the tension of underlying structures in consciousness which exist in a polarized relationship. This attraction springs from the tension and makes itself available to desire; how does the tension manifest as the pleasures of attraction? We are attracted to whatever provokes tensions in ourselves, and we feel this heightening of the tensions in us. It is these tensions that also constitute what we are at a subjective psychological level, so that the experience of pleasure of attraction is really the experience of self-tuning and self-toning, and our own growth into greater being; thus growth takes place along the dual paths of truth and power, and this growth is also what Nietzsche meant by the feeing of the will to power. But what of the tail end of pleasure? Pleasure passes through attraction into desire and then finally into release and

15

catharsis as the underlying tensions slacken and fall back into place among the larger machinery of the self, with those experiences that enabled and provoked these tensions into more attractive and desirable, pleasurable states of tuning and toning falling down into deeper parts of ourselves like puzzle pieces, allowed to fit more perfectly in place. Pleasure is this process from tightening to slackening, from attraction through desire and then to cathartic release and tranquility. It will be noticed that erotic, orgasmic pleasure is a perfect representation of this process, but all pleasures of all scopes and kinds function in this manner.

26.

Forgetting is useful in that we often, due to a failure of memory, do not overplay our hand before we could have realized that we are overplaying it. Knowledge often comes secondary to action, and a limited and targeted forgetfulness is useful in this regard for allowing our knowledge time and experience to catch up with our actions.

27.

Beauty is the coming to life of values. And the enjoyment of the beauty is also the enjoyment of the values.

28.

Others make demands on us because they do not know how to make demands on themselves.

29.

Clockwork of subjectivity 7.—Life is being wound up with so many underlying dynamic tensions that it is possible, even necessary, to release much of these tensions without ever exhausting the total state of tension of the organism as a whole.

Part 2: Logic.

30.

One of the biggest problems in the human world is that people 'care for' each other. This "caring" implies an absence of understanding and even relies on such an absence for its continued existence and utility; if one truly understands another then one does not simply "care about" the other, one acts logically according to the clear mandate that reveals what one must do with regard to the other, this knowledge coming directly from one's true understanding of the other. This also gets to the difference between love and goodwill: most people mistake goodwill for love, in so far as goodwill is paired with one or several other desirable qualities in a potential mate, with the resulting mixture being interpreted as whatever 'love' means. This is another failure of understanding, one perhaps even more tragic than the failure of understanding that is "caring". However, both of these failures resolve themselves in time, either by

18

pushing for developing the understanding the lack of which they themselves represent, and pushing in this way for the simple reason of how the repeated pains and errors that are inevitable when one acts, even with the best of intentions, upon a deliberate lack of understanding compel us to seek a higher standard of truth, a more accurate picture of reality—or by decimating us completely, in so far as that even proceeding any further according to these failures and our pathetically "well meaning" misunderstanding becomes, due to the magnitude of the lack of understanding involved, utterly impossible.

31.

People's minds are so fragmented that they cannot follow the trail of a thought for more than one or two iterations; this is also why their conversations are so fragmented, random and unproductive— not even to speak of their actions.

32.

Baring truth, hope is the ultimate balm upon the mortal wound that inflicts us all.

19

33.

Life has no final and perfect resolution, much less does consciousness have it, because life and consciousness are little more than being in a state of irresolution. This is why the individual fantasy- image in each of us is that which wields the flows of truth and power. But the development of philosophy is what allows this situation to progress forward rather than simply fragment and regress; philosophy is the forward progress of that which by other means has no capacity at all for forward progress.

34.

Nihilism as positivism.—The niceties of society exist to lessen the impact of any awareness we might have of our own state of perpetual groundlessness. And only the nihilist bemoans this utility, for nihilism is nothing but a needful belief in God carried over into its opposite, where believe is purged but need remains. Nihilism, along with all other forms of positivism, is the mournful longing for an absent 'deity'.

20

35.

Love, like every other invention of philosophy, acts as a stand-in for nihilism, mostly because these inventions do far more than simply produce "meaning", although they do that as well.

36.

What Kant, Hegel and Nietzsche did not understand.—Meaning, in so far as it is a cause, is always already an effect. This fact, through all the various ideologies of the world, is what dooms the world to failure.

37.

Even the gestalt of meaning is subject to the mandates of a natural selection, to an "evolutionary epistemology": this ground is not meaning but rather our need for meaning.

38.

Truth is nothing more than placing absolute trust in oneself.

39.

It should be no surprise that both the weak and the strong seek political power. Truth is the arbiter of this power, since while both the weak and the strong will always seek power to assert their goals and their values the weak do so at the expense of truth while the strong do so in tandem with truth. This is because truth does not mean "morally right": morality is an attempt to undermine power in both the weak and the strong, but since the weak make far more use of morality then do the strong the appearance is that morality is an attempt by the weak to exercise their power and "will to power" (over the strong). The morality of the strong is little more than reason and justice, while the morality of the weak is "moralism" and "social justice". Morality is properly moral when it is also rational and just, namely when centered in both cores of truth and power; all other forms of morality (emotionalism, ideology, sophistry and pathology for example) are mere moralism and seek only to undermine power, even the power of the weak. This is why the weak are constantly defeating their own utility and undermining any gains they may have made. Nietzsche believed that morality was a weapon invented by the weak to use against the strong; could it instead be the other way around? Morality is de-powering, which is why the strong tend to avoid it in favor of a much harder, "cruder" reason and justice, leaving the self-defeating moralities to the weak who eagerly employ these moralities without understanding how these systems do little more than limit and work against the power of those who wield them.

40.

Moral without morality.—Value and utility must be freed from morality just as care and concern must be freed from empathy, just as the larger nexus of value, utility, care and concern must be freed from "love". A joyful kindness, concern, goodwill, sympathy and helpfulness toward others are not in themselves vices or detriments, rather quite the opposite, but these too easily become corrupted into false systems of explicitly irrational psychologies and personalities. The only way to save what is truly good is to free it from the larger false systems of "moral good" that require irrationality, over-reactivity, banality and misunderstanding in order to function at all.

41.

Three core concepts.—Truth is irreducible to power, and power (will to power) is irreducible to truth. Regarding fantasy: fantasy is irreducible either to truth or to power because while fantasy expresses the truths and powers of subjectivity it is also the case that fantasy is this subjectivity, as its truths and its powers as well as its untruths and its lacks of power. Fantasy is the principle of subjectivity or the self as its higher-order self- valuing manifestation and apotheosis, and therefore is ultimately only reducible to the self as such, to "a life" and as that life. Fantasy is ultimately nothing more than an expression of the self-irreducibility of life, while truth and power both seek (and ultimately fail) to reduce life to themselves as well as to reduce themselves to life. These three concepts, therefore—those of truth, power, and fantasy ("life")—are core concepts by virtue of being fundamental. And perhaps more such concepts will also be discovered; two possible candidates for further consideration and study, then, giving nod to the works of two great contemporary philosophers[2]: value, and excess.

42.

Truth (that which is real, exists, is the case; the totality of all facts) and power (Nietzsche's will to power) are the deepest conceptual-logical polarity, entirely irreducible either to themselves or to each other; they simply are and govern everything else... everything except for life. Life is in part formulated in terms of truth and power, but life has its own, third core and axis around which it turns, namely the fantasy-image (the life-principle, inner world of experience; imagination, subjectivity, mentality, 'the self') which logic cannot be reduced either to truth or power, nor to the conjunction of the two. The fantasy-image is entirely separate from the spheres of truth and power and yet somehow it has emerged from them, or at least the fantasy-image emerged from a presiding context in which truth and power are the two cores,

---

[2] Jakob Milikowski as credited with the notion of value as fundamental, and Joseph Chambers as credited with the notion of excess as fundamental.

in order to form by emerging in this way a new, third core. The first two cores together constitute the onto-logical condition of the universe, and with the addition of the third core constitute the onto-epistemo-logical condition of Life. All life possesses (or rather is possessed by) a fantasy-image, and the more that life increases and becomes complex so too does that life's fantasy-image core also grow and become more complex. For a long time the fantasy-image only passively or secondarily expresses the dual cores of truth and power, but eventually learns how to express and speak to truth and power more directly and actively; the active and direct expression of the fantasy-image to truth is what is called understanding or knowledge, while the active and direct expression of the fantasy-image to power is what is called ethics or justice. When the metas of understanding/knowledge and ethics/justice have appeared, there we can be sure that something called "self-conscious life" has appeared, namely that the fantasy-image has developed in itself enough and produced enough of a historical textual world of contents from which it may draw new contents at any time, to come to a point of more accurately modeling its own condition as being immersed within both a universe and a life-world. The progression of this accurate modeling of its own

26

condition or "self-understanding" is what is called by the name of philosophy.

43.

Two analogies and a question.—Does the development of self-understanding in the third core, the core of the fantasy-image, imply that this core is in the process of dividing in itself with the end-result of eventually splitting into two separate, distinct cores that can no longer be reduced to one another? Is so-called sentient and self- conscious life merely a stage in a much larger process of onto-epistemo-logical mitosis? To carry this biological analogy further, it seems that the western world is passing from a prophase to a prometaphase stage in the process of its mitosis, having achieved condensation and polarization and now moving into separation. Next comes the much more active metaphase, the pulling apart of differences; could this mean anything other than open warfare and a heightening of every human conflict and madness? Perhaps if these stages continue to progress primarily in the logical sphere then the human world will be spared most of the crude display of violence and overt destruction that could easily be seen as naturally accompanying

27

this phase. But applying biological process to politics (which means also to psychology and social relations) in this manner is certainly not a perfect analogy, for the human political, psychological and social worlds are immeasurably more complex than is the microbiological world. In any case it is possible that a deep fissure in the fantasy-image core will result in the eventual production of two or more distinct human species; to employ another analogy, one from the world of finance and investing, truth and power act as the states of relations between order and disorder, or between production and a breakdown in production, and these two shifting poles of 'order and chaos' constitute a statistical spread within which a moving average converges or diverges. When the moving average is below the mid-point between order on top and chaos on the bottom we can be sure to bet on truth and power organizing along increasingly productive forces; when the moving average is above that mid-point we can be sure to bet on truth and power organizing along increasingly unproductive and destabilizing forces. As per the question posed at the beginning of this insight: does the increase in the spread of the statistical space in which the average moves imply that a deeper split and division is taking place? To precisely what extent can the core of fantasy- image (and its secondary realm of "meaning") maintain an ever-increasing self-understanding that increasingly threatens power with truth and truth with power?

44.

The world as such and the social world will always represent severe impositions upon the fantasy- image, upon our very lives, but it is also the case that the existence of the world as such and of the social world are quite necessary and even helpful to the healthful, productive functioning of the fantasy-image.

45.

Euphemisms, like the ignorances they shelter, are things that we philosophers necessarily find quite distasteful, but are things that others find quite necessary.

46.

At first technology serves an increase in power, then an increase in truth, and finally an increase in the fantasy-image.

And what is it that technology will serve to increase once it has eventually succeeded in serving an increase in the fantasy- image? It is, perhaps, impossible to say.

47.

Clockwork of subjectivity 8.—When two thinkers, two philosophers follow their respective thoughts and philosophies to their ultimate conclusions will these philosophies end up coming together or being pushed apart? Of the three cores, it seems that only truth prescribes a logical necessity for an absolute convergence of ends, while power and fantasy-image prescribe only partial convergences and even, perhaps, a logical necessity for an absolute divergence. Is the core of truth powerful enough to maintain a forcing-together of the two cores of power and fantasy-image, with respect to the necessary divergences prescribed by and as the cores of power and fantasy-image? Here the partial convergences of powers and of fantasy- images ("lives") come to the aid of truth. If the partial convergence prescribed by the cores of power and fantasy-image are each at a value of just ¼ that of the total convergence (value of 1) prescribed by the core of truth, then

30

the tripartite axis of the three operational cores will achieve balance at the exact mid-point of 50% convergence and 50% divergence. Thus each power and each fantasy may maintain its own individual divergence from the power and fantasy of others at a value of three-quarters difference; any more than this and the human world begins to fray apart, while any less and the human world begins to consolidate anew around the shared powers and fantasy-images participating in the greater organizing and unifying field of truth as such. There must also be a point at which different powers and different fantasy-images could converge too far toward each other, toward other cores of power and of fantasy-image, in which case the core of truth would begin to break down due to a slackening of the tensions between respective powers (action, will) and fantasies (life, self) causing the core of truth to lose its dynamic polar duality, namely cause to be lost any need for truth as a supremely unifying-perfecting force and organizing influence. The mental universe only penetrates into the realm of truth to the degree that is must do so; truth is only ever won by hard necessity and never by mere caprice, possibility or chance alone. It is possible that not only the irresolvable tension of the categorical, fundamental difference between truth and power but also the irresolvable

31

tension of the categorical, fundamental difference between power and fantasy are what sustain the very existence of the core of truth with respect to its being a primary core within the clockwork of a subjective machinery, to its being a core of a 'self' rather than simply being a fundamental logical principle and mere fact only.

48.

To what extent is the breakdown in human sanity and mental/emotional clarity and purpose attributable to an insufficiency of language to adequately express mentality to itself, versus being attributable to actual defects in human sanity, mental/emotional clarity and purpose?

49.

How is it possible that one has any goodwill and joyful approach to others to the degree that one also has knowledge and understanding? Can this really be attributed entirely or mostly to Nietzsche's pathos of distance? There seems to be a deep gap that this pathos cannot bridge, a point of engagement and energetic alignment even between the very different such that, despite two persons being so different from one another, it is still the case that relations form between them, relations that not only build upon whatever agreements and similarities they do have with one another but also build these agreements and similarities themselves, seek them out, construct them, and use these constructions to satisfy a certain requirement or functionality within and as each of the respective persons. And this requirement or function seems to be a need far greater and more deeply rooted than any need for a grand height for our pride or for an intimately felt distance between oneself and another with respect to our own emotionality and mentality and to maintaining our own uniqueness and 'narcissistic ego'. No, such a singular pathos of distance as well as any need for it cannot adequately explain the coupling tendency that arises between even very different people; this tendency is clearly more than simply narcissism and ego, more than a self-congratulatory pride or a masochistic enjoyment in the suffering we experience by interacting with those who in their ignorance, banality and weakness cannot help but offend and wound us. The conclusion must be drawn that goodwill and a joyful approach to others are discrete experiential-subjective forms that do not need any larger psychological narrative or system in which to participate in order to exist and persist according to their own nature. Goodwill and joy toward others are themselves deeply rooted tendencies that arise within the complex logical intersections between the operations of truth, power and fantasy, and it seems that no amount of knowledge and understanding can produce a degree of misanthropy sufficient enough to totally purge oneself of all goodwill and joy toward others, even toward others who are quite different from oneself and who would often evoke antipathy and suffering in us. So we are left with the same question we began with, "How is it possible that one has any goodwill and joyful approach to others to the degree that one also has knowledge and understanding?", and it seems that despite our brief investigation we were not able to answer it. But we at least know that the pathos of distance and the narcissistic entanglement of ego, pride and masochistic suffering/pleasure are not enough to account for it. Most likely we will need to proceed deeper into the dynamic logical inter-relations between the three primary cores, to see into the 'subatomics' therein, in order to arrive at an answer.

50.

Trust is always highly specific, and this explains why people do not trust themselves which includes why they do not engage in the ennoblement of philosophy: it is because they do not make themselves specific enough.

51.

Joy versus the deepest failure.— Power and truth each produce a kind of joy as a consequence of themselves, and their conjunction produces an especially potent and sustained kind of joy — but it isn't until the addition of the third core of the fantasy-image that the joys of truth and the joys of power begin to understand themselves, and each other. The conjunction of truth and power without the third core can be seen in the most ancient tribal humanity, humanity as barely having emerged from nature and still lacking a functioning abstract grammatical language, philosophy, science or art; it is precisely when truth and power reach their peak expression in the nature world that the third core begins to power up: while it is the case that all life possesses this third core, the fantasy-image, it is for a long time unable to function in terms of relating a proper truth-set and a proper power-set, to each other, simply because the fantasy-image is yet too small and self-consumed with its sensation and memory to give rise to the meta, a state of self-suspension and inner confusion that prompts the need for a higher-order reconciliation or what we call reason. Reason leads to understanding, and understanding systematized at the levels of biology and of psychology, sociology and the cumulative textual history of these leads to a fully powered fantasy- image that not only in potentia and in the final extreme reconciles truth and power to each other but also and perhaps even more significantly for human subjectivity achieves a true self that is full of its own contents in such a way that those contents, inherently complex and irreducible to each other, generate the highest most comprehensive perspective and meta-perspective yet possible, through which truth and power find an even higher self-expression and combinatory... power and truth. The structural existence of this highest and most comprehensive perspective, perspective self-generated from perspective itself, is synonymous with what is called happiness. It is for this reason that the fantasy-image is that which most clearly expresses and requires the introductions of immense qualities and quantities of joys into

36

human experience. This fact is often mocked by philosophers and scientists, who are too narrow-minded, cowardly and cynical to understand that the adherence to truth and/or power alone cannot succeed if it does not also pay adherence to the supreme subjectivity-existentially central power of the fantasy-image, of the third core upon which hangs the onto-epistemo-psycho-logical condition of all being. The machinery of being can only be understood on its own terms, just as an idea can only be understood on its own terms, just as sensation and memory and meaning can all be understood only on their own terms. Categorical conflations will not do when we are engaging with the most abyssal depths; and it is the false conflation of these categories with each other that is the root cause of all human psychological, emotional, meaningful, philosophical suffering, chaos, confusion, impotence and inability to bear the responsibility for self, world, life and... for truth and power, and also for their own fantasy-image, which they have learned in their pathological malformed state only how to deny and desecrate. Yet the fantasy-image is such that it can sustain even its own denial and desecration, until it becomes too damaged to continue mediating truth and power to each other; when this deepest of failures occurs the fantasy-image suffers catastrophic collapse,

37

the core shatters and truth and power vanish like soap bubbles along with any semblance of the individual who had once inhabited the space of those former cores, which have now for lack of joy been shunted out of existence.

52.

For the academics to take notice.— It is regrettable that such a vast amount of useless knowledge does not also translate into some knowledge of this uselessness.

53.

Technology threatens to co-opt the fantasy-image. The fantasy-image is tempted by technology but also resists being co-opted; is technology therefore an aspect of an attempt at reconciliation between truth and power on the one hand and the fantasy- image on the other?

54.

The will to value.—We must reform the will to power into a will to value. This is the only way to rescue western civilization, free market capitalism, individual rights, private property, and reason and law as standards. The only way to defeat collectivist ideologies is to depower their appeal, and the best way to do that is to update Nietzsche's philosophy from being one of "power as such" to being one of value as such. Why does being will to power? Because it seeks value; it seeks not only to exercise its valuing and ranking as Nietzsche noted but it also seeks to increase value as such, and it does this by seeking and acquiring value to itself. The appraisal of value by applying standards and rank-ordering differentials is only the first part, the second part is to acquire that which one assesses as being of value. And by doing this we do not merely increase our power but we increase our value—the increase of power is a result of the increase of value. Furthermore, increase of power is not necessary for increase of value, because power may even be decreased in the task of seeking and acquiring some value, for example a wealthy person may expend his fortune on the pursuit of some rare item or experience that has little or no economic transactability, he acquires it only because it is valuable to him and by acquiring it he adds to his own value despite that he has traded power for this value. Another example would be how we often trade increase in power for maintaining a status quo with regard to the values we already possess, such as to maintain the equilibrium in our personal romantic relationships or family relationships, where the 'power' is largely fixed and cannot greatly expand in either quantity or quality. Increasing value is the cause for any increase in power because power often becomes a value that is sought and acquired, but in such cases power only increases because power is being determined and rank-ordered as a value above other values.

The legal right to property ownership is the logical political expression of the will to value. Socialism and communism and their postmodern permutations stand against the legal right of property ownership, because these mere ideologies (malformed and insufficient attempts at philosophizing) are expressions of self-valuing that has determined to rank-order everything which someone else has and oneself does not have as being of no value—therefore it is clear that collectivist thinking is a form of self-valuing regression and collapse into the most basic fundament of the logic of value, in so far as the collectivist is unable to value something that is valued by others and therefore has lost the ability to equalize himself as self-valuing among other self-valuings. He has lost the will to transact for values because of his own psychological pathological malformations and traumas that inhibit his ability to apply effort to seek value. This is also why collectivists such as socialists and communists talk about workers owning the industries and business, as if the bottom of the line workers are capable of or even interested in making top level executive decisions, which of course they are neither capable of nor interested in doing. The collectivist assumes that everyone else is like himself, psychologically damaged, frail, spiteful, suffering of a lack of value, while this is usually not the case. A will to value that does not value power as such is simply an expression of heightened valuing and rank-ordering, which is a perfectly healthy state to exist as, provided that one is willing to suffer a lack of power for the sake of one's values, which is proper, but a will to value that values power above all other values is an expression of an inability to value and rank-order judgments. This is why collectivism always decays into authoritarianism: it was always authoritarian to begin with, there is no difference between

41

the authoritarian tyrant who values power (and being at the top of a political system has most likely amassed much wealth and capital to himself as a result) and the poor struggling communist revolutionary or socialist idealist who values power, who values the power to be able to take from others for the least amount of personal effort and work. When self-valuing collapses into non-dimensionality it interprets in black and white only, becomes a vicious atom of need and seeks only to convert the entire world into an extension of its own power and is not willing to form value judgments that would threaten this simplistic formula. Because the collapse of self-valuing in this way is caused by psychological damage and an overwhelming awareness of one's own personal insufficiency with regard to the deeper values that are indeed embedded in such a person, this person rejects all values that are not the value of power. It does not matter if such a person is a bottom dreg of society or a king, each will pursue the same singular type of valuing. The poor dreg only hates money because it represents a power he does not have, and he wants power, wills to power only; the rich king values money because it represents a power that he does have. Both the rich collectivist and the poor collectivist seeks money as power, but by different means and not because they view money as a medium of values exchange and a symbolic representation of value created, which is what money is, but because they wish to cancel any value that leads to the power of someone other than themselves.

The will to power appears as a consequence of the will to value, and a linear simplified will to power expresses a linear and simplified, damaged and personally insufficient will to value. We must instantiate the concept and category of value into society as fundamental, more fundamental than even power or capital, more fundamental even than 'rights'. If we philosophers and writers can achieve this then society will quite naturally correct itself and purge this error of will to power at the expense of will to value, which is all that collectivism is.

Socialism and communism are a will to power, and this entirely and completely explains their appeal, especially to young people. Socialism and communism are ideological vessels for the expression of self-valuing as power of personality. The instinctual organism, failing to have yet been properly organized by reason and ideas, by truth, instead seeks to organize itself by personality and consistent action. Power is good when in service to truth, and bad when in opposition and hostility to truth; and truth in this sense most means the truth of the self-valuing itself, which is found in application of reason to the organization of instinctual energy and the biological drives[3], which are themselves isolated and disorganized by virtue of man being torn from nature and finding himself in the position of needing to ascertain values and rank-order them. Therefore another way to defeat collectivism is to demonstrate to the collectivist how his ideology is inadequate to form a personality-power and a power of consistent action, and also to show him how self-valuing and a more individual, rational focus is more successful at guaranteeing will to power. This can be done in discourse and argument with the more reasonable collectivists, but for the more unreasonable ones can only be done by brute force of defeating them in their own terms—in the terms of power of personality and power of consistent action.

---

[3] Joseph Chambers as credited with this notion of the instincts and drives being either organized by the passive unity of the natural world or disorganized by man having left that world and instead needing to be actively (re)organized by reason and thought, "Reason, fundamentally, disqualifies the affects..." (A Glorious Risk).

55.

Collectivists (socialists, communists, radical leftists, feminists, neoconservatives and neoliberals, postmodernists) are unable to laugh at themselves because they are unable to value themselves. They are afraid to place themselves as an object of their own critical attacks. Their morbid "seriousness" masks a will to self- ignorance, because they have become the secondary expression of other values and other powers; they are valued more by that which they value then do they truly value it. This causes a severe constriction of the sphere of personality, which explains their desperation in clinging to personality-power as their last line of defense of the self. By contrast an expansive personality can move about within itself, explore, and laugh at itself without any fear of loss of self.

56.

The fact that we humans have these faculties that are called reason and self-consciousness does not mean we are superior to or better than the many animals of the natural world who we assume do not possess these faculties—it simply means that we are different than these other animals are, different in the following way: we humans have lost the natural organization of our minds, emotions and actions, such natural organization that so easily provides for the 'self' of the animal; we humans lacking the organization of the natural world must rather create our own selves, create these from out of our own ashes. We are broken, fragmented, and then these fragments become the bits and data that are "consciously" reorganized to produce what we call sentience, self- consciousness, intelligence, etc. Some humans do this reorganization process well, some do it poorly, but all humans possess a governing structure and idea, a philosophy, by which subjectivity and a self is birthed from within the fractured and suffering mentality-space. Our understanding is one consequence of this birth of the subjective through and by the powers of thought, logic, symbolic language, affective disintegration and reintegration; we humans self- value in a different method than do the natural animals, but we all each self-value and construct a self and a subjective life, a perspective, and possess the three cores. It is also possible for both of these methods of self-valuing to communicate to each other on the basis of each possessing the same three fundamental cores (of truth [what is, what exists, what is real;

46

factually the case], of power [power, will to power, the feeling of the will to power] and the fantasy-image [mentality as such, "thought", singular perspective, imagination and fantasy-desiring]). Humans and animals in nature are far more similar than they are dissimilar, and science has robbed us of this understanding and all that could be built upon it.

57.

Clockwork of subjectivity 9.—One of the three cores always takes priority over the other two, centralizing itself as the self-valuing center of the axis [power<->truth<->fantasy-image] and interpreting the other two cores in terms of itself. Each core can be actually interpreted in terms of another only to a point, and to approach thus point is health; the two cores achieve dynamic active stasis as heightened tension, each pulls on the other just enough to inspire the other and draw values to itself. It is not possible for one core to self-value the others beyond the capacity of those others to allow themselves to be valued secondarily-externally like that. The cores are perfect balance, and in this way mirror or represent the larger existential ontological world- balance that always exists at the

47

various social and psychological levels. This "balance" is a result of saturation. As soon as one change or addition is placed within a context, the sphere of that context instantly adapts across itself to accommodate that addition, that change and cause—effects are immediate and distributed automatically- unconsciously 'at the speed of light' (which is a distance) forcing extant and aggregate value-forms to adopt new techniques and presences, new actions and modes of being, all in order to account for the change and addition into the larger context, and this is the case because rash context, sphere, later, tectonics is always already saturated with itself and as itself. This is what "Being" means, to-be-as-saturated. Every strange or irrational or unpleasant or harmful action, desire, goal, will, or logos that we observe in the human world is the result of a balancing mechanism working in real-time; the three cores achieve a height and reification of dynamic tension and energetic saturation within a context of perfect tectonic balancing, indeed each core is actually such a height and 'reification' itself. By intimately understanding and accessing this level of balance and saturation, we are able to insert and manipulate causes and effects in ourselves, others and in the world. Knowledge of the three cores, of their individual natures and of their individual and group operations, is like a

48

philosophical bomb going off in the existential... forcing an even greater energetic tension, reorganization and heightened balance of the underlying values, beings.

58.

The personality of philosophy.—We seek unhealth as a means to health, we are driven to reconcile those discordant elements within us only so that these reconciled figures might again be torn apart and fragmented in a new chromatic symphony, an inner atonality recovered so that, again, new harmonies and beautiful tones can be found only because they need to be found. Need drives everything, even and perhaps most of all desire; we need to desire just as much if not more than we desire to need, for the "diseases" that plague us arise only as conditions of a healthier constitution having come to engage itself in playful experimentation, like natural selection experimenting with the genetics of the species by dictating a statistical spread of both good and bad genes in the individual. Sublime and perfect health would ultimately be self-defeating, hence the high value-standard with which we rank our vices. Here all positivism ends in nihilism, for it was always nihilism to begin with, was always the denial of a will to value that must force itself through its antithesis in order to triumph at the other end of degeneracy. Decadence is only ever overcome by the already decadent, either in thought or action or perhaps simply in the heart, in our emotions that persist because they remain so mysterious to us. The positivistic bent of modern technology is a more a consequence of this technology's recent appearance upon the human stage, than it is a consequence of some inner nature and logic of the technological itself. And science today has been swept up in this positivism, this pleasant nihilism that would rather bury the decadent than deal openly and honestly with it. Why then does philosophy today follow this downward course of science? The will to value secures itself in truth and power trough the mediating, combinatory power of the fantasy-image, and it is to fantasy, namely to imagination, thought and desire-lust that technology owes much of its modern and "postmodern" appeal. Positivistic technology and science as a will to unhealth for the sake of needing values—and this surplus of unconscious need will later translate into a surplus of conscious desire by virtue of the self-saturation of society, of which the individual is a species and remainder. Philosophers properly rise above this duality but must never lose consciousness of it, for it is one of the central keys to

50

making sure that our philosophizing remains relevant to the world at large. Philosophy must ultimately philosophize beyond itself if it is to philosophize at all.

59.

If our thought is never adequate to our truth and to our power, which is one inevitable consequence that must be drawn by comprehending the fact of the three cores and their respective self-valuings, whose individuality always presupposes any interaction and common valuing between and amongst those cores, then it should be considered a mark of superior health that one's thoughts, one's philosophy is delimited on one side by truth and on the other side by power; one's own truth and one's own power must act as safeguards and semantic limits for the reach of the fantasy-image, in order that this fantasy and image might most come into clear and defined existence. It is likewise the case that truth should be limited on one side by power and on the other side by the fantasy-image, and that power should be limited on one side by truth and on the other side by the fantasy-image, so that these three pairs of limitations end up speaking more to each other in so far as they happen to share a common limit- side. Any two of the cores might speak to each other through their commonality of being limited by the same exteriority and principle, namely the third core that is excluded from that relation between the two. Three pairs of limits gives a total of nine possible convergence points in the soul; a nine pointed star that might be seen as existing in the fifth (3+1+1) dimension, or in the dimension of time squared, time taken in terms of itself alone. The rate of change of the rate of change of a rate of change, this could be seen as an acceleration vector through which our sort of being appears. Thought must therefore learn to speak the languages of truth and the languages of power, in addition to learning to speak its own language of fantasy and imagination. Anywhere that these three languages are attempted to be reduced to a single voice, such as in contemporary science, postmodernism or in certain philosophies, would therefore represent an error, likewise anywhere that the fundamental difference of these three languages and voices are sustained in an irreducible plurality could be seen as an attempt to sing Being itself, and I believe this must have been the original form that human languages took, a form of supreme negotiations and of tri-vocality that above all else would have taken joy in the fact that it remained mysterious to itself, that "meaning" was understood to be a function of that which can be said to 'have no meaning' such as can be witnessed in the universality with which human cultures invented alien gods and unrecoverable abysses into which to throw themselves at the mercy of the always mysterious. This urge to throw oneself in this manner must therefore run far deeper than runs any of our "meanings". Philosophy should take careful note here, that it not dissolve its substance either in the world, in thought or in the search for God, which dissolutions would represent respectively a collapse into either mere power, mere fantasy or mere truth.

60.

Nihilism is not the loss of meaning, it is the redirection of meaning into useless channels. The loss of useless meaning is the opposite of nihilism, which is also the opposite of "meaning".

61.

How many people, or for that matter how many philosophers have the strength to endure the destruction of their useless meanings? Even 'strength' itself is just one more useless meaning, when it is treated as... meaningful. Such meanings are irrelevant; only truth, power, and the fantasy- image matter, and each of these attains its own reality, its own living daemon, its own self-valuing and thereby sets its own value-standard—against every other...

62.

Humans largely pass their mortal time by inventing meanings, and then by inventing clever new ways of either clinging to these meanings or of rejecting and abandoning them. What would that human being look like for which, instead, no "meaning" at all were applicable? Even Gods would tremble at the presence of such a pure monster. In the subtlest center of the axis of the three cores lies dormant this one final human power, truth, and fantasy. And it is quite possible that human physiology and psychology are not nearly truthful, powerful and fantastical enough yet to bear the crushing gravity of such a mode of being, of such an unmeasured and uncharted freedom.

Part 3: Earth.

63.

Where language fails us.—Language is always trying to adapt itself to the landscape or our values, to the intensity and immensity of the pressure of our subjectivity and to any supposed requirements that this subjectivity asserts as value-standards for itself, that it demands on its own behalf. When subjectivity is pushed to the edge of what it is able to bear as value it can no longer assert these requirements for itself, and interprets this loss of requirement as loss of meaning, which loss is then projected beyond the subject and out into the world as a threat and "personal attack", something to fight against because of the suffering it causes as we are forced to become aware of it. This is all nothing but a simple mechanism of self- maintenance, a means for subjectivity to cling to already given value-standards so that its 'ideas' might remain if not equally simple then at lest equally predictable and comfortable. The earth tolerates both the need for stasis and the need for change and growth; the seed is allowed its hard shell, only because it must succeed in breaking through that shell from within, shattering and destroying its "simplicity, predictability and comfort." Language has the easiest time speaking about either the stasis-will or the growth-will, about either "beings" or "becomings", called respectively nouns and verbs in the common parlance; but where our language begins to break down and we find ourselves unable to articulate clearly the meaning and value, the drive and will and passion and pain of the best and fire of our subjectivity within a given context of discourse or discussion—where language fails to provide a bridge from our value as subject to world value as object—there we can be sure that the seed is poised to break through the barrier of itself in order to begin the process of becoming something new. In our case this means a new kind of subjectivity with new values and new valuing powers, and this process will only be aborted if we lack the harder integrity-strength with which the seed is able to overcome the resistance of the shell around it. Language is never as hard as our integrity-strength; language is a medium of translation and transition that cannot speak where new values are quite painfully and quite necessarily being forged into existence.

64.

A big problem for philosophy is that it continues to be stuck in the labyrinth of language, where words are supposed to mean just one thing only and are praised and valued according to that lowest of standards. This positivism infects philosophy with ruin, and such philosophies are nothing more than ruins. Such positivists are unable to resist the temptation of using language in a linearized manner merely to express some aspect of their personality or, even worse, to express a mere disposition for or against something.

65.

Conquest as aesthetics.—We run from defeat more because we do not like to lose than because we like to win; defeat is a harsh limit and reality principle, and we enjoy overcoming that limit more than we enjoy reaffirming an existing strength. The earth is cruel and beautiful—and this beauty, beauty itself, cannot exist without this cruelty. Beauty is a cruelty to which we are drawn because of the limit we already are, in order to enjoy surpassing that limit. What comes after the conquered limit? Only another limit begging and tempting to be conquered. Whether in war, politics, art or when it comes to women this same rule applies. And especially this applies to our most vital and empowered knowledge and understanding, to philosophy.

66.

Optimism.—Fear of pain is fear of oneself. Self- valuing could always aspire through pain to a greater threshold and scope of being, were it not for our fears.

67.

One certain thing.—We are made out of values, out of ideas; out of experiences and out of concrete modes of experience. And these values, these ideas and these modes endure long after we are gone from this mortal sphere called life. What we call life is the propelling of values, ideas, modes upward upon the climb of existence, being into greater being, and we are but one expression of this climb toward and as the greater. What then is death, to such creatures as us? It is certain that if we enjoy and love our values then surely these make us immortal, surely do these mark us as fit for eternity. And it is the case that all joy derives from this one certainty.

68.

Why would the loss of meaning depower us, as in nihilism or in its modernist equivalent of "depression"? The loss of meaning should be praised and celebrated as the consecration of being as such, of the higher orders of existence as truth and power, manifest through our fantasy- truth and fantasy-power, revealing themselves in the shedding of layers of the superfluous and unnecessary. Why would we abandon anything that was not already of insufficient use to us?

69.

Earthy wisdom.—Existential suffering and despair exist only to draw our attention to their opposites.

70.

If we have nothing to lose in death then we have nothing to lose in life, nothing to lose in living to the fullest without regard to our mortality; this is the secret of morality, as the propensity of morality to both disclose being and to cover it over again, as said so eloquently by that strange sage and poet[4] of both the modern and postmodern worlds that we are here to live so well that Death will tremble to take us. And even more so it is not death but rather Life that trembles most at the approaching of the earth.

71.

Intelligence is required for valuing-integrity, and we can therefore be certain that all the animals are highly intelligent — whereas man appears as the sickliest of all the creatures, in so far as most humans cannot even cultivate enough intelligence to maintain a consistent value-standard for themselves. The opening up of the mental world to direct examination and

---

[4] Charles Bukowski, "We are here to laugh at the odds and live our lives so well that Death will tremble to take us."

refutation has confused man so deeply that he does not know how to set a standard, does not know how to be honest with himself when he feels that so much of himself is always in some manner of contradiction with so many other aspects of himself. Only intelligence can clear away this confusion. And there are other forms of intelligence than merely thought and cognition; for example passion, and action. If every human could embody just one form of intelligence and then achieve mastery in that form, humanity and world would come to mean something very different than they have meant.

72.

Knowledge as subservient to intelligence.—The difference between intelligence and knowledge is that intelligence always organizes the cores, intelligence derives from the cores directly while knowledge always represents a particular already- given organization, and derives from an existing organizational hierarchy amongst the cores. Intelligence is needed to organize the cores, while knowledge is what happens when one core is allowed to assume power and truth status over the other two. And then we can see how a higher intelligence will give rise to new forms and scopes of knowledge.

73.

It would not, strictly speaking, be possible to establish a logical hierarchy amongst the three cores, but if I were to attempt a practice hierarchy in terms of some overriding value and standard, even some utility perhaps, then I would be tempted to set it up as follows: truth at bottom supporting power above it, and then power supporting fantasy at the top. This is due to the fact that power is always power of something, in terms of something and truth is always "for itself", truth needs no utility or domain of application or standards in order to be truth; while fantasy builds itself as the principle of subjectivity and perspective-making, builds itself as this from both truth and power. But even though this analysis makes some sense, it is not absolute for the simple reason that the three cores are each independent and circle each other in a tectonic abyss and three-pointed axis, an ever-shifting geometry and geography in which at one place and moment a certain core will reign supreme and force interpretations of the others in terms of order being fundamental, then at other places and times this will switch and a different core will serve as the fundament. Where one core is fundamental it sets up the values of the other two, and establishes a Lagrange point somewhere in the axis. This is why human life is so confusing and impossible, because there are three possible such points of balance, and even more so because the majority of human life is not even spent in such a clear position of one core acting as standard for the others, rather most of the time all three cores are operating in part and competing against each other. A proper philosophy attempts to locate the three Lagrange points, and to identify where, why and how each point would reign over the other two, likewise the natural organization and principle of the earth is the approximating as far as possible the point at which all three cores operate adequately to themselves while not also encroaching unduly upon the others, with truth and power sharing primacy and fantasy being secondary and derivative; that is, until man arrived on the scene and reversed this natural order by placing fantasy as primary and truth and power as secondary. By reversing the natural order man was able to actively locate, in theory, the Lagrange points rather than simply aim for optimum balance with minimum remainder-excess, as nature does.

63

74.

Beginnings of a new psychology.—The body might be said to represent power as limited by truth, the emotions might be said to represent truth as limited by power, and the mind might be said to represent the fantasy-image as limited both by truth and by power.

75.

Why do we so readily sacrifice and suffer so much for the sake of a single value? From a more objective point of view this would have to be seen as a deep irrationality. On this account are humans therefore deeply irrational? Or does this propensity to sacrifice and suffer for a single value represent an attempt at a greater kind of rationality? Unfortunately I do not know which of these is the case.

76.

The pleasure of beauty is the pleasure of existence, is the enjoyment of the fact of existing as such. Beauty, which is to say vanity, has in a primary sense less to do with making oneself attractive than with making oneself coherent as a value- standard; the methods and trappings of attractiveness are a plethora of little symbols and signs that are not merely useful for aiding in mate selection and social utility but are also useful for causing ourselves to come more fully into being, and indeed any benefit to mating and sociality flow from this more primary benefit of establishing within the individual the greater ontologies of being, which is to say the setting of a coherent value-standard able to assert and maintain itself over time. The ancient Greeks understood this deep connection between beauty and ontology, with their love of proportions and their worship of beautiful forms including the highest and most beautiful form of all, that of the perfected human body. Life, it must be said, is always aesthetics, in so far as life is always self- valuing, which fact is undeniable—and the ability to raise to the highest levels both the enjoyment of and participation in this fact represents the point at which beauty and reason meet, with beauty longing for reality and reality longing for the beautiful (longing to participate in that value- standard which it already is).

77.

The basis of love.—The subtlest emotions, which are the most meaningful and forceful over us but are also the most fleeting, are so fundamental that they cannot be negotiated with others, yet because of this, of their absolute inherency they act as the perfect ground on which, if two people happen to share these subtlest of emotions in the same space of time, a common being develops. This is the basis of love.

78.

The noble humility of philosophy.—Intelligence limits itself where it becomes too much the life that cuts into life, as Nietzsche said. This is not a problem of banality but rather a problem of what is common, perhaps even simple, but a different standard cannot merely be asserted against this commonness for the simple reason that the limit of intelligence is also the upper being of intelligence and appears in concordance with a prevailing structure of truth, power and fantasy; this problem is beautiful, not ugly, because it shelters and safeguards the beautiful against the ugly, at least in the best cases which is what we are, of course, interested in. Meditating on this problem will show us why most people do not need the discipline of philosophy, for these people are already a philosophy as such, they embody and live it, they are it. And who better for the hard, hyperborean philosopher to repose himself in than in that 'common' person who is already the personification of a beautiful philosophy? We must also never assume that the limit of intelligence does not also apply, and most especially, to us philosophers. Therefore not only nobility, novelty and absolution but also understanding can be found by us in our concourse with the human world or, at least and again, with the very best in it.

79.

Clockwork of subjectivity X.—The rational mind is disconnected from the emotional feeling mind, so which is right? Which is deeper? Which one conditions the other? Even the best philosophy is far too binary to approach this question. Man is still limited by this duality, which philosophy birthed into existence. New concepts are needed, but all of the concepts still flow from this asserted binary fundament. Which concepts can come together to construct a new fundament by dismantling the old binary ground? The highest philosophy is now no more then the attempt to discover these concepts, and to put them into proper use. Every system has a remainder, even the deepest world-system that has so far conditioned all of human existence. Everything else are merely the remainders of the one remainder, the resonance of an original resonance. The one resonance is obscured by the sounds of all the others. Who is truly silent enough, who is truly deaf enough that he can hear the one remainder hidden at the bottom of the world? Only the ultimate expression of the world in totality can forget the world entirely, so that only this one thing remains.

80.

The child of humanity.—Children always redeem the sins of their parents, either by purging or by absolving them; to purge the sin is to live and embody it more fully so that the sin grows and sinks deeper into the earth, where it decays and feeds the unconscious soil of the future, while to absolve the sin means to cleanse the future of it by living and embodying the exact opposite of that sin, namely by converting error into truth which here means to convert unconscious into conscious, to 'spiritualize' the body of humanity.

In striving for perfection the child either resolves the error or resolves against that imagined state which would oppose itself to that error, which is another way of saying that the future embodies a single virtue and value: hope, which is not accidentally the last to leave the vault of mystery and contradiction, for it is upon hope that all mysteries and contradictions hang. And to fail to seek perfection would be merely one more error seeking its... perfection. The child will never receive the forgiveness and understanding it seeks from the parent, just as the parent will never receive the child's hope, although both may strive together for this resolution. It is not the child who is the remainder of the parent but rather the parent who is the remainder of the child, for the child is a higher-order resonance in a sea of lesser sounds that it cannot comprehend; that in its purity and singularity of self with which it gives voice to the multitude of discord that has grown up upon the confused world of things the child reaches the same stars that the parent has long since given up aspiring to and adoring, because while it is the purpose of the child to strive to create such heavens it is the purpose of the parent only to strive to create the child. Humanity has for the most part still failed to learn this lesson, and still strives to live in reverse of itself, still trying to place the remainder prior to that of which it is remainder. The flow of nature works in one direction, the flow of mind and the mental universe works in quite another direction.

The first moment of philosophy is born in the absence of hope, while the second moment of philosophy is born in the rediscovery of hope. There has yet been no third moment of philosophy, because philosophy, like humanity, has yet to see the value in caring for and placing above itself its own children, its own core value and future which is also to say its own very best in both truth and error, in strength and in weakness to which philosophy, again like humanity itself, can never truly aspire to. Where the parent merely creates the child discovers; where the parent merely discovers the child creates—and if humanity can be said to be the child of philosophy, then it is only the child of humanity, the third moment of philosophy, that could ever hope to be the redemption of philosophy—...The children of our lusts, of our desires, of our values; of our ideas and ideals, of that which we already are and always have been; of the best in us,

70

also of the worst in us; of that which has no name and of that to which all of our names return: here we encounter the self-value in raw, unmediated and pure form, which is to say our self-value. It does not matter if we "have" this value so long as it is our value. For to win the value often leads only to a different value, and this is because of the fact that having and being are not at all the same thing.

81.

Aristocratic valuing.—Democracy fails because it is not possible to actually reverse the relationship between power and money. Democracy is the idea that the obvious and always existing relationship between money and power can be reversed so that the poor and the powerless and the stupid can somehow be that toward which money gravitates... yeah, no. A more silly Christianized idea can hardly be imagined; and it is no wonder that democracy in practice actually degenerated quite quickly into consumerism.

At best democracy allowed some new channels of power and value to sprint up in society, but this is more a kind of aristocracy than any kind of democracy. Money does not "vote", it simply follows value. The powerless man wanted value he didn't have and so he invented democracy, the ultimate Greek-Christianism, but even Athens had the good sense to keep democracy little more than a pragmatic system of managing the interests of those who have power (aristocracy). But then the mob took over. Socrates gave the mob a voice, and they killed him for that because the mob can never truly learn to speak and never wants to. The mob never understands that money follows power, hence why the mob became Marxist. Marx as basically Jesus 2.0. How long after Jesus did his thing that Rome collapsed? How long after Marx did his thing that our civilization will collapse?

Consumerism is subjective compensation for slavery. Aristocracy figured out how to lie to the mob, with "elections", and thus forced a higher degree of subtlety and sophistication upon aristocracy while also forcing an elevated will to power upon the mob. The mob learned how to love the feeling of the will to power, and finally believed that power was within its grasp or even that it had attained power; this feeling/desire (which is entirely false, as the mob never really had power of course) expresses as consumerism, and aristocracy tolerates the conversion of economy from mob-peasant farming and tradecraft into mob-peasant consumerism. This set up a new layer between mob and aristocrat, the layer of the industrial capitalist and top tier businessman. Huge corporations mediate between the mob and the aristocracy. Consumers just want to be told lies about how much power they have, and corporations sell them the marketing products and experiences to do that; meanwhile these corporations always maintain loyalty to true power, namely the aristocracy, and money continues to migrate toward value which means toward power in all its varied forms.

Aristocracy only had monopoly over a certain kind of power, and its deficit in other types of power is part of why consumerism works so well as a new economic model: money (like women, and indeed it can be said that women are, in terms of the feminine nature, a sort of "living money") is attracted to power, and the more elevated in the mob can possess certain kinds of powers that aristocracy does not typically possess (in part because modern aristocracy is only a shadow of what it used to be), such as literary or creative artistic or industrial scientific powers and all these imply, therefore modern capitalism is able to provide upward channels for certain more intelligent and visionary people to find success and money in the economic world. Large businesses and social institutions co opt these individuals and put them in service of maintaining aristocracy.

The aristocracy has lost none of its will to power, but it certainly has lost much of its former intelligence and "high breeding", while the mob has actually increased in its will to power. Consumerism holds back the will to power of the mob, as democracy itself can no longer hold back the mob's increased will to power. Marxism (Jesus-ism 2.0) may yet sweep the world with a new religion, a neo-Christianism that knocks aristocracy even further down the tectonic hierarchy of nobility (if not of actual power in a political sense) and increase the will to power of the mob even more; since aristocracy is always what structures social, political and economic infrastructure and systems this will mean another dark ages, for the same reason that the dark ages occurred when Jesus finally killed off Rome. The dark ages are a period of slowly rebuilding aristocratic infrastructure systems into something that can provide consistent power and value, namely is able again to attract money to itself and thus build itself back into stable existence.

By reaching new heights of will to power the mob actually enlightens or at least ennobled itself, as a kind of unconscious growth substance on which it now consumes in new ways, self-consumes (inverted, because early and nascent, self-valuing). Check if aristocracy or the mob have been on the rise; unconscious is climbing toward the light of consciousness. Aristocracy is going to be trapped as "the body" of a new humanity, at least this is the root of the Socratic-Jesusist-Marxist plan.

Morality is a weapon the strong invented to use against the weak, by making the weak "moral", but this has begun to backfire as even the strong are trapped in this net. The net is only a means to another end that end being the elevation of the mob into nobility. "Mind" does not need to become a body in order to elevate itself. Technology is currently nothing but a way of maintaining consumerism, thus of holding back the will to power of the mob, but technology will increasingly become a new body in which the aristocracy is frozen in service to the "mind" of the world, the mob-master that will live the new dark ages. Crazy humanity with imprisoned leaders in ivory towers, forced to "manage things". Not forced by physical force but by moral force.

This new growing will to power of the mob is an awesome thing to behold, and make no mistake that these magnificent displays[5], indicative of this growing will to power, are always eminently moralistic which is why they must couch themselves in images of raw power and in an overt consumerism, both of which the mob believes to be more or less "non-moral".

---

[5] Iggy Azalea, Goddess, official music video

Part 4: Value-Daemonics.

82.

Music is a good example of the pure daemonic excess that is human language, thought and feeling: before the song begins it could be anything, it is literally infinite in potential, but as soon as the first note is laid down a limit is formed, a boundary around what is possible and what is impossible. The few notes first created develop a logic and an aesthetic that further limits the space in which the song can develop; it is within this increasingly severe limitation that the song is able to produce meaning, and indeed this is how all meaning is formed, perfectly daemonically as Chambers says, the infinite excess differentiated by limitation and then those differentiations set to limit each other in moments of time, which in fact is what produces what we call time. The method of differentiation requires always new differences forward in time from those prior, and the method of logic requires these new differences building from existing ones must be further limited and bound in their scope of possibility, so that a process of differentiation over time narrows and begins to converge upon what we call the meaningful. Meaning here is simply the fact that a point is reached in the convergence process such that differentiating the entire priori process itself becomes easier than pushing forward to a posterior difference in the same existing process: when the differential chain can no longer draw enough excess into itself to derive a next stage difference from itself the chain stalls, but only for the moment it takes for the existing differentiation points in the chain to begin to differentiate from each other so that the chain explodes like a supernova, its inner heavy elements spreading around it and becoming available to other differential chains in their own respective excessive processes.

83.

We invent moralities so that we can overcome them.

84.

The daemonic explosion and blowing apart of love that we see in contemporary culture is a sign that the underlying excess beneath the differential chain of experience constitutive of what we call love and the meaning of it has become frustrated and unable to draw excess into itself sufficient to carry the daemonic process forward one more iteration, so that now this chain explodes and the inner heavy elements of love are released into the world, which means into both societies and psyches, and become available as free objects to our desires and to the broader consumer economy. We will have to wait and see if the inner heavy elements of the long history of the production of love are strong and self-valuing enough to continue the logos and ethos in a forward direction; without the overriding symbol, without the idea of love, these free elements may decay and dissolve or they may begin to spin in the darkness of the soul and draw other elements to themselves, create a mass and a gravity, and start a new world process and thereby find humanity a new fate. When a major daemonic chain explodes this leads to loss of the old meanings, but can also lead to the beginnings of new daemonic chains producing new meanings.

When a major chain such this, such as love, explodes this is like a long worm blowing apart into a dozen smaller worms each of which now beginning to grow on its own. The most truthful experiences of love will lead to the largest and most stable growths, new daemonics as the underlying excess is recoverable by the new spinoff processes of differential chains forming themselves from the fragments of the old major chain.

85.

In death the body disintegrates into its elements, these elements dispersing and becoming available to other organic processes, and this same process occurs in our minds and in human history with regard to our ideas, our sentiments, and our meanings. The only difference is that unlike with disintegration of the body we do not die when a mental process disintegrates. Disintegration means that a differential process linear in time explodes and differentiates itself laterally in space; thus we see also that "a body" is already such a process of space being produced from mere time, a point of stability as excess recovery along the spatial dimension and which becomes stable in time by learning to daemonically self-value itself as a 'cloud' of free elements each negotiating excessive chains and processes, so that the body is produced as the governing thought that structures this cloud of pure excess-objects, and remember too that the excess can only produce objects and can only come into existence by being limited and subtracted from a larger context in which it is embedded, thus when a daemonic chain explodes this produces little spheres of self-contained excess having formerly been extracted from its larger context and set against that context in productive differentials. We see that evolution is not actually what produces or what explains organic bodies, but rather it is the case that evolution simply describes one aspect of the process by which bodies form, namely that aspect associated to environmental pressures and to how genetic mutations in replication act as a mechanism for this... but in order to fully explain what bodies are and why they exist we would need to account for all of the daemonic differential chains, their production of structure-inducing excess extractions and the reification of these extractions into 'objects', and the periodic explosions of daemonic differential chains once those chains become too narrow and constricted to produce new iterations of object-ifying differentials. Such an analysis would be capable of revealing the specific traces and causal histories behind every human idea, sentiment and indeed behind everything that we find

meaningful, everything that is actually meaningful to and for us.

86.

The difference between emotions and mere feelings or

sentiments is that emotions are the explosions of daemonic

differential chains: when confronted with radically different

experiences and with the convergences of existing meanings

within ourselves, convergences in new and different ways by

virtue of the uniqueness and significance of presiding events

around us, existing differential processes in us that produce

our thoughts and feelings encounter a strict limit and temporarily

abrupt, stall and all of that forward momentum of the chain is

compressed and released outward as free excess-objects

scattering throughout the soul. We feel this scattering of objects,

objects that are themselves basically pure excess condensations

but are otherwise invisible to us and unable to be experienced or

felt directly because are always already trapped as the

continuum-points along a specifically delineated, daemonic

differential chain; we feel this scattering as what we call

emotions—the emotion is an infusion into feeling of both far more potent and expansive meaning and significance as well as of a sense of the excess as such, which is a rare experience for life to directly encounter not only the products of its excessive nature but this nature and excess directly; the production of new emotions, new emotional depths, and the massive increase in the felt and known significance of life to itself, this is what emotions are and represent. To stack true emotions like these upon one another in time, rather than merely in space as is the case with the historically codified and stabilized lesser emotions that are common to all people, would produce a meta-level continual explosion of greater significance and true excess into the soul. This must be associated with the beginnings of a true heroic daemonic[6].

---

[6] "The question as to what extent the reconciliatory and regulating power of man's art, of the visionary heaven of the world of the ideas, is capable of reaching into this utmost tension of the soul and transforming the sickly profusions of life into genuine strength is one as yet unanswered; the daemonic individuality can only be transcended by heroic near-divinity when that utmost tension of the soul is grasped, when the abyss between Death and Eros is fathomed and circumscribed within the border of the human will; when that abyss is moreover charged with the energetic tension of a struggle,

87.

When we make choices we are exercising our freedom. We do not know that we are free because we happen to make choices, rather we know that we make choices because we happen to be free—and to make a more difficult, risky or harmful choice exercises our freedom all that much more deeply and significantly than if we had instead made the easy, safe and more comfortable choice.

---

when an opposition of conceptions is properly conceived within which thanatos and eros might wage war with one another and in so doing generate the practical contradiction through whose excessive forces the human being might be drawn aloft in deathless, heavenward ascent across the abyss, a possibility which might be rendered poetically, out of Foscolo's Le Grazie, *molle armonia temprate, o Dee, gli affetti de mortali e i pensier*: the thoughts and feelings of man, the movements of the heart and of the soul, are not so opposed, for each has as their ultimate object nothing other than death, embracing one another in the strange harmony with which love succeeds in tempering a long life." Joseph Chambers, *A Glorious Risk*

88.

Language is a pure daemonic process, with every sentence
consisting of the forcing together of distinct concepts in new
ways to produce a unique differentiation that maintains its
difference rather than collapsing it to any kind of synthesis; the
very meaning of the sentence is this anti-synthesis, and no
meaning could ultimately be possible if our language instead
forced differences together in terms of each other: what gives
meaning in the proper sense is that each term in the sentence, each
such term being irreducible as itself, is combined with each other
term in the sentence in ways that prolong and extend
differences in space and time, literally pushing something new
into being. The very fact that terms can be put together like this
proves that consciousness works daemonically as a process of
excess-expansion. When an excess space is expanded in this
way, such as when a sentence is formed out of various
individual words, the various concepts comprising the sentence
feel themselves growing as the sphere of their significance and
reach extends due to the extending context of the expanded space
of the sentence, yet also feel themselves growing smaller and

condensing due to the fact that as the context space increases the relative size of any given term in that space gets smaller. This is how concepts become individual in the first place, they must be forced into individuality by being 'extracted' from a much larger context in which they are forced to participate meaningfully, so that finally a name can be given to this extracted segment; such operations are far in the distance of the human past, yet every human today had to go through such a process in infancy and childhood to learn how to speak. As the mental space expands outwardly it crystallizes inwardly, as the context in which differences can be meaningfully applied increases those differences themselves become more individual, acquire their own character and distinct meaning, develop a "feeling" for themselves in opposition to everything else in mentality, and then by crystallizing in this way become available to new processes of daemonic differentiation as these terms enter into new even more limited contexts with each other. The massive and irreducible tension between the most precise terms in mentality and the larger space of mentality as such is what gives consciousness its reality. The more precise we are in certain terms within ourselves, and the more of such precise terms there are within us, the larger and more expansive we must become in order to meaningfully contain that precision. Meaning itself is properly just this expansive tension irreducible to either the smallest or the largest relatants within and as mentality.

89.

Sexuality is a truth process, such a process that is exploited by nature and by human societal dynamics for purely utilitarian purposes but is really, in itself, a direct expression of daemonic expansion around the increasing individuation of the key terms involved, namely two people whose very existences become participatory in a daemonic movement by which individual terms are heightened to a maximum precision by being brought together in a larger state of tension that envelops those terms and concentrates their respective differences and individualities by making them participatory in a far greater scope and context than otherwise would be possible. Sexual attraction itself is an example par excellence of daemonic differentiation, and even our more basic desires and pleasures flow from this larger daemonism of the human consciousness. The human consciousness is daemonic, it is literally constituted by and as a daemon as such, and therefore extends itself outward in more derivative and specific iterations of itself, such as our desires, by forming new daemonic relations within itself. All the sensory input in the world would mean nothing to the human being if this being were not daemonically integrated across the expanse of itself, because it is this very state of being integrated like that which forces incoming sensory stimuli to become participatory in processes of meaning far beyond what they otherwise would be capable of accessing. Every sensory input potentially indicates something far beyond itself, to man, and indeed indicates many such things far beyond that given input, as the space of potential indications for any given stimuli is limitless, or rather is limited only by the size and integral complexity of the daemonic consciousness to which a given stimuli becomes a sensory input. Sexuality, desire, pleasure and sensation are all literally daemonic processes and extensions or expressions of such processes, and nothing besides. As truth itself is pursued, therefore, one inevitably develops in and as this truth-seeking process a character of 'sexuality, desire, pleasure and sensation', namely truth itself to the philosopher becomes increasingly sensational, pleasurable, desirable and sexual just as each of these becomes more and more truthful, more and more participatory in the overall process of the daemon.

90.

Nature has co opted the beauty of life, of the daemonic consciousness, for the most banal and ugly purposes but life remains beautiful nonetheless; the daemon is eternally patient and waits for an eternity if necessary, waits for developments in its environment to occur that allow it to become free from the shackles of the mere natural world and to begin to exist in an environment and context of purposes that accord with its own nature alone—humanity is this very development, and nothing besides.

91.

The phenomenological-analytic poisoning of meaning occurs when the accidental and purely external logics of mere utility, which logics are always present to some degree in the larger world and nature, impose themselves upon the human daemon in such a way as to assert themselves as primary over this daemon and the 'world and nature' of the daemonic consciousness. Man is this daemonic consciousness and therefore cannot stand being limited like that, being constrained as if the mere accidental, banal and external were somehow the more significant onto-epistemo- psychologically primary component of man. It is true that man lives in an accidental, banal and external world just as it is true that man is subject to the various utilities and purposes of such a world, but this fact in no way imposes itself fundamentally upon man nor speaks fundamentally to who and what man really is. Real meaning always originates from something about the daemon itself, while false meaning always originates from something about the external world; we should learn better how to distinguish between these two types of meaning, and if we could do so then much suffering would be avoided. Indeed it is the case that suffering and pain as such are little more than this same sort of confusion, a conflation of one type of meaning with another (the real with the unreal) and the imposition of an external dead world upon the already living daemon.

92.

A great human nobility is found in the humility and quiet strength with which man accedes to accepting the external imposition of the world upon himself, and indeed this pain is also used by man as another limit within which to differentiate himself even further. Yet the character of the differentiations, their respective qualities, are far different depending upon which is doing the upper limiting, either man or world. Humans can limit each other and thereby act as worlds for one another or, absent this, can simply allow the world itself to act as this limit—and it is within the higher context of being limited by other people that the being-limited-by of the world takes on its richest character and value.

93.

Man often acts as if he were the smaller term in a much larger daemon, the daemon or mind of the world, and therefore submits himself to "the world" without question; man acts as if he were merely one individual term and concept within a larger daemonic consciousness, so that man could only come more individually into life by being subjected to immense pressure and tension by the larger world-mind in which he exists, and yet such a situation is entirely not the case. While it is true that the world often appears as if it were a daemonism, as the "world daemon",

91

and just as it can appear as if the world self-values, it is as little the case that the world is actually capable of self- valuing as it is that the world is actually capable of being a daemonism. If man believes he is but one value within the much larger self-valuing of the world, or if man believes he is but one individual term within the much larger world daemon, then man will necessarily shrink before himself and fail to attain his fuller daemonic, self-valuing stature. Why does this assumption exist, the assumption of the primary status of the world over man? It exists because it is possible to see the world in this way, and also because it is often more difficult for man to see himself in true terms than it is for him to see the world in untrue terms.

But why is this the case? The world of appearances and illusions steps in where man is unable to attain a truth standard, and where is this more the case than with regard to himself? Therefore "the world" is naively interpreted as such a standard while man to himself is interpreted as mere appearance, superfluity and as so much that is accidental and lacking in proper and certain substance. There is an inherent bent in man that resists this tendency toward a falsifying interpretation, and it is within this inherent bent that is located man's dignity and his power of self- love and joy, which are the same thing; a dignity and power from which all other of man's dignities and powers flow. Until man learns to see himself as not only the primary term but also as the larger situation and equation itself, which he is, he will continue to remain in slavery to the world of mere appearance, accident and arbitrariness.

94.

The study of history is always a study in interpretation, and not simply of those in power but rather it is the case that the study of history is interpretation as such. To reduce history to dates, places, events, people and to so many "obvious causes" is an act of gross falsification that would not pass muster in any philosophy. A philosophical study of history consists instead of an interpretation of the interpretations, a study of what have come to comprise the studies of history thus far, and this is not merely "hermeneutic" but rather quite the exact opposite.

95.

What can be said about the value of the daemonic consciousness?
A deeper and more fundamental question   has   hardly   ever
been   asked. The daemonic depths of valuing must be explored
to give a clue to how this question can be answered, and firstly we
must state that the daemon posits value to itself, for itself, and in
terms of itself, but it does so by extracting values from the
world around it and converting these from mere stimuli into sense
impressions as input into the mental universe, which also includes
the body of the organism since both share the same kinds of logic
and work in tandem with one another even as both also
maintain their separations from each other; when a stimulus
enters the mind or the body (and the body is simply an
extension of the daemon, as is the mind also) it is converted into
the language of that particular daemon, it becomes a term in the
larger expansive/differential process that constructs chains of
terms in antithesis to each other as the space of one term is made
to intrude upon the space of another, but cannot actually enter
that other space fully, and so a mutual tension is formed
between these terms and one signals and influences the other
without ever giving rise to unification or synthesis between

them. Unification and synthesis are retroactively imposed upon daemonic differential chains, by the processes of other chains and by virtue of how a given chain can be exploded by failure to progress its momentum forward in 'time' (each successive iteration of the chain), either due to the chain encountering something that truly arrests and stuns it or due to the chain reaching the limit of its ability to convert that excess which it is into a next step iteration of difference because of how narrow and minute these iterations have become. When this occurs the given terms of that chain explode outward around it to the degree of the inner tension and excess of that chain, which is now being compressed in space, and these exploded terms come to constitute more or less free objects that become available to be taken up by nearby chains and valuing processes.

Each chain values, but each chain is also valued, and each term values (in terms of that which it is, namely how it was originally formed by extraction from a larger context and codification in a given delimited object-range) but each term also is valued, by other terms and by other chains. These shared valuings form the basis of what we call meaning. If we are to get to the heart of the issue of value with respect to daemonic consciousness, and to the heart of the issue of the daemonic consciousness with respect to value ontology and self-valuing, then these threads of meaning- potential will need to be uncovered and examined up close, like putting one's eye right up to a spider's web or, better yet, looking at a spider's web through the zoom lens of a high-definition camera. Our philosophies must be this camera, must be this lens turned upon the most complex, interesting and significant of all possible subjects—ourselves.

96.

The only meanings that are true are the ones that come from the daemon itself—which means from your daemon; the only meanings that are true are the ones that come from self-valuing itself— which means from your self-valuing. All other types of meaning are worse than useless, no matter the impression they may give.

97.

Every emotion communicates a depth, every emotion is precisely such a depth and the feeling of the emotion extends exactly as far as how deeply the emotion goes within us; the emotion exists only as far as it is able to go within us, within that substance which we already are, and no farther. Into what is this depth extending? It extends into the daemonic differential chains that comprise the latticework of what we call the soul, and as the emotion pushes into this substance remembrance is evoked, like fire: the emotion evoked enflames itself as its heat and friction causes daemonic chains to explode outward releasing free objects, these objects acting like neutrons in an atomic weapon, causing a cascade that we experience as "memory". Why is the experience of a forceful emotional memory given as something painful, in addition to being pleasurable? Pleasure and pain mix in this experience, but why? The true meaning is buried deeply in the daemonic self, as literally part of that self, so in order to experience that part of the structure as a memory and emotion that part must be exploded from its place in the overall structure of the self, released as a free object. This allows the meaning to be experienced directly and individually, to be valued by us and to self-value itself, but the price of doing so is to cut that experience out from its structure and to damage that structure a little bit. When the free object of the emotional memory fades from our present conscious awareness, as it inevitably does and usually does fairly quickly, it is not as if the original position in the structure corresponding to that emotion is now gone, rather it that position is now a little bit faded, has now lost some of its color and vibrancy; every emotion, every significant remembrance is an act of copying something, of making a duplicate of an original and much like the process of genetic transcription and replication it is also the case for the transcription and for the replication of memories/emotions that over time these fade in clarity, most especially in their emotional clarity and in the clarity of their true meaning the more they are copied into conscious awareness. When true meaning fades it is all too easy for false meanings to gather, and for us to value using false meanings to bolster the loss that we feel, the fading of the emotion, and these false meanings are simply any meaning that comes from outside of oneself, that does not correspond originally to the daemonic self-valuing that oneself is. The loss, which at first is simply the recognition of time but later as the memory is repeatedly experienced becomes the recognition of the loss itself, a self- consciousness of loss itself, which means damage to the structure of the self, is the source of the pain that we feel in recollecting even the most beautiful and significant of our emotional memories.

Treating our memories with a bit more care, being gentler with them and not forcing them into such direct recollection is one way to help memory maintain itself with less loss of coloring and less loss of the intensity of the true meaning from which the memory and its emotionality has been derived, but this also means that one's present moment consciousness will not be informed as significantly by those structures in us—we must trade some stability and lack of pain in the present for the ability to properly experience our own true meanings in the form of deep emotional remembrance, and if we are not willing to make this trade, if we prefer instead to avoid this pain more than we prefer to understand it then a different trade- off has already been made and the philosophical, daemonic, self-valuing structure in us and that is us will fragment and begin to dissolve eventually anyway, but for very different reasons than if we had been able to will truth and depth for their own sakes even at the cost of emotional pain.

98.

One degree of freedom.—Time fragments and dissolves all things, most especially the mind, consciousness, and the self, but we can at least choose the manner in which we are to come undone and exit this life for the eventual destination of oblivion. Will we value life, or will we value oblivion? Eros, or Thanatos? This choice is always present in everything we do, in every moment we experience, indeed we make this choice as what we are in every moment, our actions, thoughts, feelings, words, motivations and desires all reflect which of these two choices we have made. We can disappear within life and as life, which requires embracing a sadness of loss far deeper than would be required if we instead were to disappear within oblivion, for there is no sadness in oblivion, only the numbness of nothingness and lack—or we can disappear within oblivion anyway, because we are too afraid of the pain of losing life, and to make this choice means only that we have already lost life but are unable to acknowledge this fact, which is to say that we will continue to lose even what little life we have left. Only courage before loss braces the self against time. Pain and in particular emotional pain is not something to be avoided but rather something to be embraced and understood, because these pains communicate ourselves to ourselves, the impassioning of the deep structure within us with truth-movements that long for the light of day, long for life and fresh air; even as they begin to perish, even as they

100

become aware of their mortality just as we become aware of ours, these parts of ourselves shine most brightly and display the most beauty right as they come into this greater understanding, for knowledge always ennobles and beautifies in so far as that which is known is itself noble and beautiful. The capacity for the beautiful and noble, for life itself, to embrace its freedom in mortality, to will life even in the face of oblivion, is one degree of freedom that can never be taken away from us, nor from those parts of us that mark themselves the very best in us.

99.

Every emotion, every significant moment has many different possible flavors and qualities through which it can be experienced, even the same emotion and moment amongst two people will be experienced differently because of these differences in flavor and quality, which are differences in perspective and in valuing. An overall context is what tends to change the flavor and quality of a moment, and what is a person and a perspective if not "an overall context"? Even the same emotion can communicate a thousand different subtly distinct qualities and nuances in feeling and meaning, given a thousand different situations and contexts, and this is true both with regard to ourselves alone as well as with regard to taking place between ourselves and others with whom we have developed an emotional connection. One primary function of human consciousness in the social sense is the ability to recognize when we are sharing an emotion, and its quality or flavor, with another person. In other words the other person is able to bolster our own emotionality and to expand and clarify the range of possible emotional senses and qualities we are able to experience and come to know, just as we are able to do this for the other person. This is among the most fundamental bases of friendship.

100.

Cultivating vantage.—Sometimes the depth of our insights outstrips our ability to write these insights, at other times the depth of our writing outstrips our insights. A philosopher must know how to balance these two depths and know how to tip the balance one way or the other as the situation calls for; we must compensate for the limit in both our insight and in our writing, or else one depth will swallow the other and produce too much time, which means we will need to catch up to ourselves and as a consequence lose much of our time, insight, writing and...

depth. Sometimes depths descend down into the abyss, at other times they stack up to the heavens, and we should be especially careful not to fall in love with either of these progressions. Philosophy, like life, is pushing back the limits just enough to secure truth and power to each other thus emboldening the fantasy-image in us, which means to stimulate the daemonic tensions with new valuing. Every great writer, artist or philosopher knows about this dynamic within himself and has learned over time and by trial and error how to set the equipoise this way or that way, constructing vantages by playing depth against depth in the great abyssal soul of the mental universe. Daemonic consciousness and self-valuing already presuppose the attainment of such a state, such a carefully placed existential tectonics. But if we cannot fall in love with this or that depth in us, with these various insights or with our art or writing, what then may we fall in love with? The vantage itself is perhaps the greatest temptation of love to us, that we might sit and reflect on eternal things and allow this reflection to permeate our thoughts, emotions, desires and most especially, perhaps, our personality and our actions. A completed human being, or at least one in the process of completing himself or herself—perhaps this is what we most long for, perhaps this vantage alone is what ultimately tempts us from one abyss or another back into life.

101.

Either side of ignorance.—Philosophers are far too complacent, apologetic and appeasing; they ought to make much more of a loud and consistent complaint against all of the non- philosophers for failing to understand or read their works. This would be among the best ways to cement our philosophies, and a philosophical preference and capacity in general, into the masses: by forcing them to deny philosophy and to defend and value their ignorance we have already won against that ignorance. In order to summon the capacity to defend and value ignorance they must either employ some truth and strength or they must decay even further toward the nothingness that is the ignorance they already are—regardless of which path they end up taking we have created the conditions by which it is now more likely that at some future point they will come into philosophy, only because they must come into it on either side of their ignorance: show them their ignorance and they will at least muster the courage and self-valuing to defend themselves.

102.

The necessity of existence, a simple argument: Premise 1: Something exists, and we know this for certain, based on the existence of our own experience and based on the fact that in order to make a statement like "something exists" then logically something must exist to make that statement.

Premise 2: We know that because something exists it is not the case that nothing exists.

Premise 3: The principle of sufficient reason (PSR), which includes the insight that something cannot come from nothing.

Conclusion: By combining these premises we get the conclusion that it is not the case that nothing has ever been the case: we know that something is the case now, and we know that something cannot come from nothing, therefore nothing was never the case. Ergo, something has always been the case—existence, as the existence of at least something, exists by demonstrable logical necessity at least given the fact that something exists right now, which is undeniable.

103.

Everyone wants to see themselves differently than they are, but only from the outside; they externalize any valued supposed differences from how they truly see themselves, projecting these onto others as vanity of vicarious perception, when in fact to truly see oneself as different than one presently is one would need to change how one sees oneself internally, not merely externally. To want to see oneself differently from within, this is what most people avoid at all costs, and for good reason: the change from within implies that what is viewing the change is also changed, therefore the standard of value-appraisal may also change and this change could be small or very great, with no way of knowing in advance. Who really wants to change if it means changing, in some unknown way, how we actually value and appraise ourselves both as we are now and as we will be? Two peaks of personality risk each other upon this height, namely a supreme self- confidence and a supreme self-hatred, each of these vying to be the emotional force that ultimately catapults us over the threshold of willing the internal value-change. It is perhaps a mark of nothing but our character, which runs deeper than any of our secondary value-appraisals of ourselves, which of these two personality structures will prevail. Yet in order to avoid the possibility of either of those structures prevailing, most people never desire to change their internal view upon themselves—whereas the daemonism of philosophy provides the greatest self-valuing security, therefore we philosophers do not have that problem.

104.

In school young people focus on play, socialization and partying over education because it is play, socialization and partying that tend to comprise the capital-logic of the adult world. Kids and adolescents are acting out the relationships and behaviors they see in adults around them and projected by the world at large. Conservatives often bemoan that kids care more about friendships, social dynamics, fashion and popularity than about more "practical" and "real" concerns yet it is "friendship, social dynamics, fashion and popularity" that run most of the adult world and which govern nearly all capital-logic.

105.

Men tend to want, whereas women tend to want to want. This means that men tend to have straightforward desires and to act on those desires, whereas women tend to desire other people to have desires, and then women will hope that these other people's desires correspond to something that the woman herself can also enjoy and participate in. These two types of wanting are not strictly speaking male and female types, but are simply two different forms or methods of desiring, and men and women tend to cluster more on one type or the other. Children begin in the first type of direct wanting and then branch out into the second type of wanting (other people) to want, and eventually migrate toward one type or the other in their finalized personality. Women have desires just as intensely as do men, but the way women go about seeking and obtaining their desires causes them hardship and stress that men do not tend to experience; a man will suffer hardship and stress for his values because he will desire these values and attempt to obtain them, but this requires hard work and effort, and even with these he may not obtain his desire, which will frustrate him and cause some suffering, but a woman will suffer the hardship and stress of others around herself whom she values, and she values their valuing of her just as she values her own valuing of them—it is the case that a woman's complexity of valuing/desiring is not yet known, because of the difficulty of penetrating this ouroboros-like structure whereby a woman values others in so far as they value her, yet she values herself in so far as she is valued by others whom she also values.

This difference between the two types makes sense when viewed from the perspective of evolution: men sought to control the world in physical and mental conquest, to obtain direct values, while women sought to control men for the purposes of reproduction and rearing children in security. Thus evolution formed two stable valuing-types and distributed these amongst early humans for the purpose of balancing out human self-valuing, with male psychology tending to take up the route of direct valuing and female psychology tending to take up the route of indirect valuing. Today it is not a question of blindly obeying one type or another based on our gender, but instead it is a question of identifying within ourselves both of these two types, for both types are indeed present to some degree in most people, and in identifying them in this way we should see the benefits and detriments of each type, and which type rules us so far. If flaws and problems are detected then we should switch our type to a better one, which for us philosophers most likely means that we should rediscover how to directly value, how to want things without complexity and without caring what other people want or if their wants correspond to our own. As far as we are speaking of philosophers, I believe this applies both to men and to women, in so far as there are some women who can properly be called philosophers. And if "philosopher" too is somewhat of a spectrum of distributed qualities and capacities, namely the philosopher is not only someone who exists qua philosopher but who also exists on a continuum developing toward greater philosophical heights, then I think we will see more female philosophers in the near future. I mean properly female philosophers in the true sense, which means both that these women will be properly, truly feminine and properly, truly philosophical. Obviously this represents the destruction of "feminism" in its modern formats, which destruction is something that only women themselves can accomplish; only women who aspire to philosophy, to truth, power and fantasy and to their own self-valuing as the feminine psychology and physiology, would be capable of dealing a death-blow to the ugly, anti- philosophical monstrosity that feminism and postmodernism have become. This monstrosity is the other side of the freedom which women now enjoy—that as Nietzsche said, the wolves of our nature also yearn for freedom when we give even only the singular best in us a newly expanded scope of freedom. It is not possible to free one instinct without ultimately freeing all the others. Hence the will to power battles in culture and society today, hence also why it is important for the philosopher or aspiring philosopher, rather this philosopher be male or female, to probe his or her own depths of desiring-method and learn about the type of wanting that he or she is possessed of, and then rediscover a strength in the opposite type as this but especially to revalue the type of direct wanting, direct valuing-seeking without regard to manipulating the wanting of others to one's own ends. The philosopher must be a monster of truth and self, with indifference outstripped only by self-valuing and daemonic depth.

106.

The greatest evil is that evil which has convinced itself it is good—which has forgotten what evil is and means.

107.

Nothing fakes depth like true shallowness.

108.

What Marx got backwards.—It is not capitalism that is a means to communism, but communism that is a means to capitalism.

109.

Which human trait spells the most harm for humanity in the long run? I would say it is man's ability to ignore and pretend as if he does not know something that he does in fact know. To deliberately ignore truths that would be unpleasant for him to acknowledge in his thoughts, actions and emotions represent a grave and perhaps mortal threat to the human future. It is for this reason, among many others, that cultivating philosophy in the world is still one of the most important tasks at which we can labor. The conversion of even a single mind to honest perceiving and thinking, which means to philosophy, is an immeasurably great gain for man and future.

110.

Things are gilded with a 'mystical appeal' precisely where there is no more significant depth or greater meaning to be found in them—or where none wants to be found. Mysticism and religious imagery work on many levels, but where this ethos has overtaken the climate of an entire place or culture we can be sure that there reigns a great banality of superficiality. A prime example: India.

111.

The means to depth.—The world is a will to power, yes, but even more significantly it is a means to depth. Truth, power and fantasy came together to produce the necessity for these means, as life is already embedded in tectonics and cannot afford to sink deep roots. We might make a quite Nietzschean revaluation here and reinterpret the will to power as the very fact as such, as well as the practical consequences as such, of the means of depth.

112.

Apathy of subjectivity 1.—There is a deep apathy in the human soul. This is perhaps a leftover entropy from the natural world or at least from the non-living world, which still forms the basis of all living worlds; the trick seems to be to channel apathy into certain areas of our selves in order to keep other areas more or less free from apathy, and the danger is that apathy would spread beyond the confines we have imposed upon it. It is therefore very important to be very apathetic in a few areas of one's self and life, so as to provide for a sufficient release of the apathetic force that cannot be removed and otherwise cannot be managed or held in check. A highly developed and rational society would already have many such areas laid out as options to choose from and would endow these areas with meaning, value and a given respectability. This would ensure that the other more significant areas are left relatively free from the pernicious influences of apathy. And a society that has already begun to seriously doubt this "given respectability", namely a society mired in Marxism and postmodernism, is well on its way to freeing the underlying apathy as an uncontrollable explosion and scourge upon the most significant, important and essential areas of itself.

113.

Apathy of subjectivity 2.—There is always a balancing going on in the soul whereby finite quantities of energy are made to wax or wane as demands are made upon certain areas in ourselves and in our lives. This is why when we exert additional effort in one area other areas inevitably suffer; this is a consequence of the simple space and time realities to which everything is subject. And subjectivity itself: the most carefully refined and delimited mechanism of this self-balancing type.

114.

Apathy of subjectivity 3.—If people cannot be inspired by greatness, happiness and possibility as such, then they can at least be inspired by risk, hazard and pain.

115.

Apathy of subjectivity 4.—At a certain point we grow tired of even our own insights—or these grow tired of us.

116.

The original discomfort or psychological error observed must be dealt with either directly or indirectly, which means either immediately or down the tectonic chain at some point in the future. If not dealt with immediately then it becomes likely that the discomfort and error will spread to others who originally had nothing to do with it, in large measure because of how people tend to ignore problems and then shift the blame, for sufferings caused by unresolved problems, onto other people or circumstances that only happen to be related by a coincidence of closeness in space or time—hence the highly unconscious and secondary-arbitrary nature of so much psychological suffering and human conflict. Much better would be to honestly and immediately identify problems of error or discomfort caused by other people or circumstances, and for that matter caused by us as well, and remediate these just as quickly so as to not allow the psychological/social deficit to spread as an unconscious excess throughout one's experiences and relations. But this would require identifying blame and fault, which is something that most people are entirely unable to handle. It would seem that only philosophers are ruthless and direct enough to be sufficiently honest about errors.

.

117.

The moodiness of artists.—It is true that the world has become too serious, too somber, too stiff and full of boredom and slavish habit, but such rigidness is required as a compensation for frivolities of the higher-order, required for elevating humor, jest, lightness of all sorts into a higher tectonic plane upon the existentia; first comes the somber serious, then comes the singing and levity, because these latter must be cultivated as a capacity of resistance against all manner of weighty and burdensome things in the soul felt intimately as requirements and necessities. We should stop bemoaning the rising or falling of this or that capacity in our souls or in our societies, for the central importance of these capacities

117

alternates over time and will always do so. Understanding this alternation allows us to set ourselves above it, secure our own depths and resist the suffering and despair that seems all too inevitable for us given our awareness of the (alternatingly) trivialities or brutalities of the present moment and world around us. Humanity is a work in progress, an artist's dream upon the canvas of life and it is an undeniable fact that the artist's temperament can always be counted on to be, like his creations, necessarily alternating in scope and focus, and a work in progress.

118.

Ethos anthropos daimon.—We must change our fate in order to change our character, and this is exactly what we have always been doing all along.

BOOK 2: DAEMONIC TENSIONS

Part 1: Regarding the concept of Daemonic Tension[7]

Take the example of the "disability bureaucracy" and the Ontario

Human Rights Commission and Tribunal that Jordan Peterson

talks about, namely the fact that universities today bend over

backwards to issue disability accommodations and force

professors to accept these without question even if the

accommodation is unreasonable and undermines the integrity of

the learning in the class. That is just one example, the whole

transgender pronouns and 200 different genders thing would be

another. This push for 'equality' is like one side of a daemonic

tension, with the other side being the idea of standard-setting and

of maintaining a hard integrity without regard to extraneous

factors or to how someone feels about the processes of

maintaining integrity and of setting standards. But this goes far

beyond this context of education or transgender pronouns, of

course. The temptation is to come down on either side of these

issues, more abstractly on either the left or the right politically,

---

[7] "Daemonic tension", as used by Joseph Chambers (*A Glorious Risk*).

119

"accommodations" vs. "hard standard setting" respectively (loosely speaking), but in fact it is the case that coming down on any one side is actually the problem, or rather, the problem is the fact that *the issue is beyond either side*. The human tectonic world is fluxing and testing the limits of how coherently it can exist, so that these sides of the tensions will get stronger and stronger in resistance to each other until something breaks and the tension retreats, and then the two sides collapse back into a more passive and benign, unconscious version of themselves. Right now the tension is high and increasing, Trump and his win are evidence of this. What I find interesting is that these tensions are becoming more conscious now; we are all aware of them and this is obvious by the fact that we feel compelled to come down on one side or another, and even if we personally do not come down on a side it is the case that other people and society at large, including our employers, will force us to at least act as if we are coming down on a side. It is not possible to remain neutral unless we are mostly isolated from society and from any personal consequence, such as losing our jobs for example. Note that being neutral does not imply ambivalence or being overly agreeable to any one side, rather it involves actively and openly speaking *against* each side when it is proper to do so, namely it involves remaining *openly*

120

and actively unaligned to any one side. Such is the proper position of a philosophy, of course. But regardless of that, most people do take pains to avoid offending others, and would simply not talk about these things if they don't have to.

Despite this agreeableness and ambivalence, as well as despite the overt pressure to conform to one side or the other (or rather perhaps *because of* such things as these) we are all becoming more conscious of the tensions now and these tensions, being more conscious, are having more of a direct impact. Trump was a lightning rod for this, or maybe he is a manifestation of it and as manifestation caused the tension to mount even higher. But the tension will eventually subside again, be subsumed back into the unconscious. People will forget all about these issues as certain ideas born from these current tensions will be accepted as given truths. But we are not there yet because the issues themselves are not clearly defined and delimited enough to allow those unconscious ideas to be born... so basically the whole process is: 1) differences exist, 2) the larger contexts are insufficient to clarify those differences, 3) given differences as given ideas (previously forged 'unconscious ideas') begin to rise to consciousness, because of those errors of insufficient clarity, 4) as

121

these ideas rise to consciousness their errors are exposed, the irreconcilability in the ideas themselves is no longer able to be ignored, 5) daemonic tension increases between the poles that define a given set of ideas, 6) people feel compelled to choose one side of the tension or another.

That is where we are at right now. Eventually the tension will break, at which point it will be 7) differences are again subsumed into the unconscious as new given ideas are created and become sufficiently functional to society. When that happens then such ideas are also made psychologically palatable for the individual, and he stops needing to think about them; they enter and restructure some part of his unconsciousness.

There are truths on both sides of these current tensions, and both sides are each vicious and brutal in their passions and methods. I like this, for it is very Nietzschean. Postmodernism is definitely a serious threat, but even if it were to triumph in a significant way (break down and subsume the other side of the daemonic tension) this would only cause that overall tension itself to break, which would return thinking back into the unconsciousness on these issues. The danger is that the postmodern side would win a clear victory here, break the other side, and then the newly created ideas that enter unconsciousness would be formed entirely from the postmodern side of the daemonics, but I cannot see that happening because it is simply not possible for the postmodern side to win in that way, and the very existence of the heightened tension right now is evidence of this fact. So actually there is no danger at all, this is all one large Nietzschean daemonic process and one side could only win if it has already lost, if it has already collapsed the tension and thus lost its own power and purpose. Postmodernism as post-Nietzschean, post-WWI and II ideology is just a sign of this overall tension and of how that tension has not yet been able to be broken; too much is conscious right now, in a human sense, I am sure Nietzsche would have seen it that way too. These people today cannot handle all this consciousness and they are seeking a way to resolve much of it back down into the unconscious, as given ideas that cannot be questioned. But in order for that to happen the ideas that are eventually born must actually be able to structure both that unconsciousness of the individual as well as the structure and functioning of society, which obviously they cannot do right now.

Another interesting observation is that even if postmodernism were to win the clear sense I mentioned, all this would do is return it back into the unconscious, totally depowering it and subjecting it again to the fire of the entire unconscious monster in which errors merely live as errors, remainders in the structures, namely even the worst of postmodernism would be made benign if it were to win, and eventually its errors, to the extent they were still problematic, would again be pushed back up into consciousness again and the whole process would repeat.

The difference between "having uncompromising or clear standards" and "accommodating a disability" is an interesting issue because in a way it represents and symbolizes the whole underlying 'metaphysical' struggle. Unconsciousness birthed a dimension of consciousness from within itself in order to force new means of structuring itself, and then that consciousness enters into daemonic tension with those conditions which caused its existence, and even more so the reasons behind the given consciousness enter into daemonic tension with those reasons behind the unconsciousness which ultimately birthed that consciousness itself. Most of life and human subjectivity is unconscious, namely we are highly structured and automated in our bodies and minds, this structure we have being a consequence of this whole daemonic evolutionary process having been played out over millions of years. Philosophers would perhaps always be aberrations within this process and regardless of at which point in the process we happen to find ourselves. This is because philosophers actually *return unconsciousness to consciousness*, which is a reverse of the primary process of the unconscious birthing consciousness for the purposes of that unconscious, and is also and therefore not something most people want to deal with. Certainly it is not something society can tolerate in any large quantity or for a long period of time.

Art is a part of the process that represents the movement of ideas from unconscious to conscious, and from conscious back to unconscious. Art is born in the philosophical impulse to raise to conscious, to free the ideas which means to see and be bothered by their errors, and then art matures as part of the returning movement of consciousness back into the unconscious, as new ideas are created which are able to regulate the unconscious in terms of those just-released errors. Artists do not just create works of art, they also create emotions, attitudes, subjective patterns; they *create ways of being*, ways of motivating and of feeling, ways of experiencing and ways of valuing. The specific works of art in painting, music or whatever else shepherd these newly created "affects" or subjective modes of being, like how people feel for example, also what they are able to think about and in what ways, and it is these "affects" that successfully mediate the frenzy of the error-ridden old ideas (which frenzy is the cause of the mounting tensions in the daemonics of society) with the reconfigured forms of those ideas that have again buried those errors, or perhaps even released some of the errors, namely allowing them to return to unconsciousness.

Modern technology is interesting therefore because it can be seen as a growth of infrastructure upon the artistic domain. All of our technology today basically ensures that art will be permanent; visual and audio technology is a form of permanent art-making that suffuses into the very stuff of our lives, into the economy, into everything really... it is the becoming-art of the world. This permanent status of the art domain negates the old function of the art domain which worked in clear developmental cycles, in evolutions as fits and starts, with clear beginnings and endings to each cycle where such endings marked the creation of the new ideas that were returned to the unconscious. Now, art and economy are fusing together and this is transforming society into

126

a permanent mediation and negotiation between the conscious and the unconscious, so that no more true cycles are possible. Only smaller cycles can now occur. Trends, "memes", etc. Before modern technology, one artist or an artistic movement would entirely reshape the material situation of society, redefine new forms of art, invent new media and techniques, and all of that radical creation was what allowed for society to respond to the artistic cycling of returning the ideas back into the unconscious... this doesn't seem possible anymore. Art itself has now become the frenzy, the ideas have actually entered the medium that is intended to work on and reform them. Technology is the coffin in which art dies, because no artist and no art movement can totally transform this technology or its material basis... so it is no wonder that modern technology takes on the outward form of being "artful". Technology is the compensation for the fact that art no longer serves the purposes it once did, because it is technology itself that has killed off art. Ironically though, this technology also frees art to everyone, "everyone became artists" in the modern world due to modern technologies. And we are required to become artists if we are even to relate to society as it now is.

So we can say that art itself broke apart, it used to be one thing and now it is infinitely lesser fragments. The human soul is infused with a small bit of the nature of the artistic domain, rather than as in the past every person was either a direct living manifestation of the entire ethos and will of art or an outsider standing beyond that ethos while being passively reformed according to it. But all this also marks a situation in which the daemonic tensions cannot be released, because it was always 'art' that released them, and it was always the fact that a few artists could direct the rest of humanity like pawns, totally changing the game in a literal, material sense. Technology created an infrastructure of existentiality and economy that is unable to be changed like this, unable to be revalued at its base, so now the new artists are either the creators and manipulators of this technology or are the passive consumers who are drawn into this technology as art-ifacts of it. This is probably also why there aren't really any truly great artists in the world anymore and have not been for some time.

Ultimately the tensions should be maintained and even increased, since this is the mechanism by which all things exist, as that active daemonism which through irreconciliation with itself comes to produce new dimensions in its being, whereas when the tension is largely or suddenly released this results in war; war then leads back to a state of new tensions, but much is always lost in the process. Currently every idea and belief is peaking toward a fever pitch, attempting to discover its own value-core and thus fortify itself logically and psychologically so as to continue to exist in the growing sea of idea-powers that define society, economy and politics. Our task might be to help maintain the tensions and help them to increase, in part by accepting the individual self-valuing of others even and especially when this individual self-valuing is at odds with some others, when the individual position, will, value, sentiments and thoughts are in no way "universal" but conform to an individual's own subjectivity and that particular scope of interest and truth which such an individual is presently working through and within. Maybe only philosophers ought to be "universal", although there does exist a universality underneath every individual's subjectivity and self-valuing daemonic consciousness and associated irreducible tensions, this dimension of universality being what has already been forged in the past as the true tectonic foundation of the most given ideas and emotions. Even those most given ideas and emotions fail to achieve universality, of course, yet they act as representations, living symbols in Chambers' usage of that term as applied for example to

129

the idea of God, and these symbols indicate and link us to the deeper foundation of meaning and facts/logic which is really our access to the universally true.

Emotions are always values in terms of the past, this is precisely what emotions are and in so far as these values have proven useful enough to survive over time and become solidified into the physiological structure of our bodies we all possess this basic constitution of sentimentality. Thus if one wants to value in terms of the future one must in a sense deny these emotions, at least to juxtapose them with new feelings from new vintages of thus-far unimagined values and ideas. In this way we can learn about the values from which we have come, and determine which we would keep and why, likewise which should be abandoned or subsumed under new "feelings". The fact that existing emotions are based in the past does not mean these emotions are "bad", certainly, but neither does it mean they are good in terms of tomorrow. Likewise morality is an intellectual codification of these emotional histories, to help them better live and breath more deeply in the realities of our existing lives. Morality, in contrast, imposes an existing standard upon the deeper emotional-historical value structure, which is why all artists and great people of thought or passion have always to one extent or another flouted

the moral customs and scriptures of their times. This is not an

attempt to deny but rather to free the emotional excess of the

underlying foundation of values. The price paid for moral

certainly is always a narrower range of feeling and an intellectual

strangulation, which quite obviously no free soul can long

tolerate. Rather to feel from the perspective of the future, this

would produce new and striking emotions, which may one day

become codified into new moral ideas and customs. This is the

primary function of art, also perhaps of philosophy.

Good and bad represent two sides of a daemonic tension, although

the labels 'good' or 'bad' can each be used to identify either end of

the tension so long as, once assigned, the other label is then used

to identify the opposite end of that same tension. In order to look

past the concepts of good and bad as well as past the moralistic

and sentimental meanings that come with them, which meanings

also exist and bear tectonic potency despite how they are being

used to conceal or perhaps to at least mark with a mere image that

serves to identify only insofar as it also conceals, one must know

the intimate details of the *particular* opposite ends of a given

tension to which the concepts of good and bad have been

used/assigned. It will not do to have little familiarity with the specific persons, situations, actions, motivations or domains of knowledge, etc. that are all together a ground from which each side of the tension draws its existence. It is often the case that each end of the tension will have very different grounds, although these will share many surface and formal characteristics with one another, which is easily explained given that the two ends are indeed two ends of the same tension.

When one sees into the deep causal realities of the two ends of the tension it suddenly becomes clear that good and bad have been applied *retroactively* and for the use of making one or both ends more identifiable and useful in some way, for instance to organize a psychological and/or social response, to build something else in another tectonic frame, to produce from the situation something that can be wielded as a weapon in some other existential conflict, etc.; when intimate understanding lifts the labels of good and bad, however, it also becomes clear that their assignment to those particular ends of the tension could easily be reversed, the good and bad could be reversed and come down on the other side. Indeed this is precisely how each side of the tension experiences itself, as the good, and determines the other side as the bad. *This is what good means: the self-identification of one side of a daemonic tension.* Despite that this is how the tensions work, from the outside the ends of the tensions are always assigned to more static and absolute labels of either good or bad, and this is one reason for so much human conflict. If we are honest we know that the other side of any conflict sees itself as 'the good', just as we do see ourselves as the good (even if the other side knows in some ways it is also in the wrong, just as we too always know about ourselves there are ways in which we are also in the wrong), but we would still tell ourselves that, despite how the other side sees itself as the good, it is *really* the case that we are the good, and this idea gets reified into a status approaching objectivity. This is the moralistic lie that not even Nietzsche had the courage to expose, he chose instead to expose the lie of Good and Evil but remained silent about the lie of good and bad.

It is also the lie of good and bad that prevents us from seeing the tensions. The tensions are everywhere yet we do not see them; we feel them indirectly as if feeling the wind that we cannot see and yet which forces us here or there; in terms of the daemonic tensions we feel their effects on us and thus identify the sources/causes of our motives and motivations as "feelings". Just as we identify the wind by how it feels when it impacts us and not by what the wind really is, really looks like or really means, so too do we identify our own inner universe not by its actual reality and significance but merely by how it makes us feel in any given moment.

Value Ontology explains how each being determines its own goods and bads, and the goods and bads of one being may or may not align with those goods and bads of other beings. In addition to this fact, every being is composed of daemonic tensions both within itself as well as between itself and other beings, and the particular determinations of good and bad that a being makes (according to its own self-value) cannot be pushed through these tensions in order to redefine or over-determine those tensions; this is most easily seen with regard to the tensions that exist between beings, but is also equally the case when it comes to the tensions within just a single being, and this inability of the good/bad self-value determinations to be pushed through the tensions is due to the fact that the tensions themselves are not 'moral' in any sense at all, although they are usually labeled as such, but more precisely because a being does not "own" (control, manage, possess) those tensions out of which it is comprised much less does it own those tensions that exist between itself and other beings (indeed this is why a being does not even own those tensions which directly comprise it, for such tensions have always existed before that being itself existed, and extend in both space and time far backward and outward beyond the boundaries of that being itself; that the tensions are "of the universal" in a way that the being itself is not, or said another way, that the 'being itself' is only a manifestation of many daemonic tensions and of the various convergence points between them, like a symphony of strings in constant state of tension and in which each string is always being pulled a little this way or that way, affecting the others around it).

The notion of morality, at a deeper level, means to indicate the fact of the assignment of determinations of goods and bads, which is always done from within a self-valuing framework, and then once achieved may be expanded out into derivative frameworks of agreements between multiple beings, which is precisely how the human world is organized to a large degree; yet this morality and the self-valuing reality of the determination of goods and bads (which includes the setting of standards by which interactions and experiences are encountered and able to be encountered) that it comes from, or rather that it refers to, is not sufficient to reveal the web-like reality of daemonic tensions that we are at all times bound up within and bound up *as*, and this is because the tensions are not themselves 'beings' but are like tectonically maximally reified statements *about* beings, which is to say that the tensions sum all of the facts of a given range of existence respective to said being for which those tensions are truly daemonic tensions, and concentrate these facts into something like an aspect which, by being concentrated in this way, become causal to and causal for that being in new ways, allowing it a more stable existence by either fortifying one dimension of its freedom or fortifying another dimension of its unfreedom, its certainty and immovable grounding. We are built from logic and facts as from the irreconcilable and irreducible states of opposition that maintain between these logics and facts, and from how in time the progression of the development of logic and facts into larger more derivative, 'meta' forms works by daemonic principle of irreconciliation and subsuming whereby oppositions are brought close together to produce more force of tension that then produces a reaction in those things which are thusly opposed, causing them to harden as points of resistance against the other side of the tension and draw the overall tension more firmly into existence; the result of such a process is sometimes called a dialectical synthesis, but in fact it is much closer to a triadic-tectonic breakthrough which revalues the logic and facts in question, consolidating the underlying tectonic reality of the original tension itself as of the two polar ends of that original tension which have now been either "resisted" or "overcome".

Countless such tensions in various states of triadic development exist all around us and within us, indeed it is out of such a myriad of tensions that 'we' even exist at all. Many such tensions have been formative in that past of that which we now take for granted as structure or function, as 'hard reality' and more importantly as fact and as meaningful. Thus it is the case that beings, by self-valuing, make use of the existing remainder reality in which those beings suddenly find themselves upon having come into existence, and beings will immediately begin setting their determinations of goods and bads based on holding themselves as the standards for such determinations, which means: based on holding that which they are as the standards for such determinations, and this "that which they are" is precisely the *myriad of tensions* that, as stated earlier, we do not see but rather, like the wind, feel in its effects on us when these tensions are moving under the surfaces of the salient realities of our experiences. Beings must assign their own goods and bads and make determinations about the goods and bads of other beings in order to be capable of relating to and negotiating with other beings as well as to gain more insight into the nature of one's own goods and bads through comparison and acquisition of knowledge on the subject by whatever sources are helpful in that, but the actual daemonic tensions which comprise the sub-structure of being/s cannot be described in terms of good and bad (much less in the terms of Good and Evil, as Nietzsche already pointed out), not even in terms of those specific goods and bads that a being has determined itself to be, for itself, the case. There is one insufficiency here when applying the moral impetus to the making of determinations about others, and then there is another different but related insufficiency when applying the moral impetus to the making of determinations about oneself. The insufficiency or the error is seen in the fact that the moral criteria and the moral need are acting from outside of the tensions and not from within them, and thus in order to relate anything about those tensions to themselves these moral tendencies must collapse the underlying tensions into mere caricatures of themselves—they must complete a reduction of the target object of the idea or knowledge in question, which is sought either for its own sake or because it is useful somehow, into a mere image of itself that, and

138

this would perhaps be somewhat less problematic if not for the
fact that by reducing the tensions into an image in this way only
the surface characteristics of those tensions are recognized, while
the deeper characteristics are ignored and buried, indeed must be
deliberately buried in order for the larger "psycho-ontological"
process of image-making and image-using to even be adequately
functional to that being itself who performs it. While these images
still become functional to us, and cover over many errors and
difficulties that we cannot know, being remains truthful to itself in
so far as it always maintains intimate connection to those tensions
which are formative of its own daemon: namely that while it is the
feelings that are the form in which initial encounter with the
tensions takes, also a form of ignorance, it is also the case that we
are attuned to the tensions on this feelings-level and over time
have engaged in a process of cultural and psychological
refinement and expansion of this world of feelings, increasing our
sensitivity and the scope of feelings we are able to feel, until what
are called emotions have appeared. The emotions are like meta-
feelings that convey the tensions indirectly as both the fact of
them as well as their meaning and significance to us.

We can compare color to the variety of our emotions: just as it is absurd to ask about a "qualia" with respect to colors it is also absurd to ask about a qualia or an essence when it comes to emotions. Subjectivity does not somehow present these things (colors, emotions) to us as if by some mysterious apprehension of an unknowable qualia by which the uniqueness and meaning of the experience is encountered, rather subjectivity *is* these things, literally they (colors, emotions; also ideas) are the direct and literal differentiations as such of the underlying daemonic tension-excess. Color is not our experience of a representation of a difference in electromagnetic wavelengths, rather *color is the experience of this difference literally and directly without any medium or filter in-between*. Strangely it had been imagined that colors (or emotions, or ideas) are things that represent some other, more "real" reality and thus we are left to suppose that the more real reality is not accessible to us and that some medium within subjectivity must be (we don't know how) interposing itself between us and the reality, causing for example the color we see as red to correspond to or represent that particular spectrum of electromagnetism which it does in fact represent. Thus our experience of red is supposed to have some mysterious "qualia" which accounts for why our subjective experience of this thing "red color" is what it is rather than something else, as pertains to experiencing one little spectrum band of electromagnetism — we can already see the absurdity in this position since it is now easy to understand that the color red is literally the experience of a spectrum band of electromagnetism and nothing besides. The "color" is what this experience of that range of the electromagnetic band is to us: the brain needed a way to represent differing wavelengths of photons for the purpose of differentiating objects in the visual field by what type of surfaces those objects have and what materials constitute them, which is what determines the particular wavelength of a photon bouncing off that object, and therefore we simply experience such differences directly as visual differentiation as such, which is what we have come to call color. Color does not "represent" those differences and color does not possess or represent some mysterious "qualia" of subjectivity; color is the difference as such experienced directly as vision, and there is no mystery as to how one color came to "represent" one range of electromagnetic spectrum or why "red looks red" and not like something else. "Red, yellow" etc. are just words we have come up with to represent the differentiation that evolved in our visual systems with regard to identifying objects by how their surfaces reflect photons with various wavelengths, the

141

"colors" are literally this differentiation and nothing besides. Such "problems" as "why is red red" or "qualias" are nothing but fictions invented by poor philosophers.

So of course this same principle (it isn't even a principle, it is simply how these things happen to actually work) can be applied to emotions, and also to ideas. Our subjectivity is not somehow producing this amazing surrogate inner reality of perceptions and sensations that are wholly unique to this subjectivity and somehow correspond to other things in reality (although the problem of correspondence is much less devastating to this type of position as is the problem of how and why those particular subjective 'perceptions and sensations' took on the form and "qualia" they did) from which they are not only separate in space but also in fundamental categorical type. This absurd idea owes itself to many of the philosophers who, like Kant for example, were not subtle enough of thinkers to ascertain that experience is direct and that any error, limit or lack in any of our experiences of any kind whatsoever is not an indication of a fault in experience generally or as such but is rather simple an indication of a fault in that particular experience itself and occurs for a particular reason. If one were to add up all of these 'particular reasons' for the faults

142

of any one experience (or for all experiences, for that matter) then the "problem" of subjectivity would vanish entirely into a perfect understanding of what this subjectivity is, how and why it is delimited as it happens to be at this one moment in space and time, and from where it may go in the future to continue to move into its own progressive development, expansion, freedom, self-knowledge and self-refinement. Also the philosophers are not entirely to blame for this mistake of understanding that phenomenology and epistemology so often demonstrate, since it was from the theologians that much of the impetus for this sort of thinking took hold. And of course the problem could be traced back to Plato, although I do not much blame Plato for it since he was far more of a capable and subtle thinker than would have simply fallen prey to such an error rather than attempting to explore and explain it, as difficult a task as that was so many years ago when he was doing it, likewise when these attempts were actually attempts to e plain something about the mind and consciousness rather than of the larger reality, and he intimated the deeper connections there but was only able to put such an idea into a far too poetic and unscientific language, owing to the particular time in which he lived and also, quite obviously, to his very early position in the history of philosophy.

143

The emotions are the experience of something directly, just as the colors are the experience of something (spectrum bands of frequencies of light radiation) directly; so what is it that the emotions are the direct experience of? They are the direct experience of a large segment of the daemonic tensions that underlie human meaning and subjectivity as a great excess, as an excess out of which our individual subjectivities have taken shape as a specific delimitation cut out from that larger excess. The larger excess holds in itself and in potentia every possible delimitation, every possible "subjectivity". The emotions are our direct encounter with certain more fundamental and causal (to and for us, also to and for others) daemonic tensions that took shape in the human past because these proved useful for codifying a particular set of meanings and facts in such a way as to allow humanity (that society or tribe to which the developing emotions applied) to become more defined in terms of those relevant meanings and facts. Thus the meanings and facts which proved most significant in this way were elevated into primary status within human subjectivity, by being impressed into the physiology of the human body as a particular organization of certain physiological responses/changes in the body our direct feeling of

144

those responses/changes, and then collected together and united as one single "feeling". The feeling itself, in this case the emotion, is our direct experience of those daemonic tensions to which those relevant meanings and facts apply: first the meanings and facts are formed into daemonic tensions, namely made livable to the world, made "physically" real, then those tensions are imposed upon and as the human body. Thus over time the human body comes to be remade in the terms of those truths which are most significant for that human body itself, and our understanding and feeling (emotions) is the direct experience of these truths, although of course our languages and reasoning are not yet sophisticated enough to properly represent all of this reality to us as a fuller, more conscious kind of self-understanding. Our consciousness simply is this understanding already, lacking very much "self-consciousness".

Part 2: The Depth-Experience

1.

I realized today something quite significant and surprising: people simply want to sink themselves into some depths, any depths at all will usually do. It is as if we get our psychological energy and motivation from sinking into these depths, whether these depths be things like sports, math, science, crime, friendship, love, philosophy, music, TV shows... these are all just depths, to man. We do not tend to abide surfaces very well.

Another significant and interesting depths is drugs. Drinking is a depth for me, whereas drugs are depths for others. Drugs are an easier depth because you can simply "push a button" and get there, just ingest the substance and that's all it takes. Food itself becomes a depth, with drugs. I know that I drink alcohol to get to a certain depth-point because my other preferred means to depths aren't sufficiently accessible to me anymore, most of the time, so I am now theorizing this is also the case for other people too. The mundane phrasing of this idea would be perhaps "trauma leads to

146

mental illness", as more recent so-called trauma informed care models in psychology and drug abuse are saying now… trying to make 'the system' less traumatic, to smooth out the differences and sufferings, always accepting and embracing and never "judging", using a "harm reduction" approach rather than punishment models, etc. All of this sort of thing is reflecting an unconscious understanding that the person's preferred or natural depth has become estranged from them and thus they have turned to different much easier and more reliable depths, namely in this case to drugs.

I suppose people need depths because they aren't good enough for themselves. Nietzsche called it will to power but I don't think it is that, it's more like a deficiency in each of us. What Nietzsche calls will to power I would call an existential need for sinking oneself into depths which need emerges due to a structural deficiency in our selves or "souls". Yes, the soul is damaged in these two ways: 1) it is born into utter lack, existential lack, it cannot know itself or be itself, therefore is driven to depths in which it can sink itself and better escape itself as well as better encounter itself in those depths, and 2) once the soul discovers those experiences which are the natural depths that are best for it, best meaning that such depths maximize the gaining of self-escape and the gaining of self-encounter in just the right ways and combinations such as to make life most meaningful and endurable by mitigating most precisely the effects of those specific sufferings, pains and deficiencies which said person happens to possess in his or her soul— once such natural experiences and ideal depths (e.g. love, or an artistic passion) have been discovered they are somehow rendered inaccessible to us, due to the profound banality and chaotic, indifferent nature of life and the world. Life in the basic sense is just a stupid survivalism, and this logic still ensures quite strongly even in us humans today. Even Nietzsche got swayed by this "stupid logic" and tried turning it into a fundamental philosophical idea, being blinded by Darwin as he was, since Darwin's theory was in Nietzsche's own time still quite novel. Yes it is true that a survivalism is always present and always necessary, but it is also stupid, namely is un-philosophical (with Chambers, who once defined 'stupid' as that which is un-philosophical). The need to "survive" in order to exist is at the core of the existential problem of depths that I am outlining here.

We find our ideal perfect depth and then we are denied it, or we find it and sink into it and then it turns out not to be ideal after all, which just means that, again, we have been denied our proper ideal depth. Thinking that we have found the ideal depth but being denied it is slightly different than thinking we have found it, sinking into it, and discovering it wasn't ideal after all; but in either case a denial has occurred and we are forced into sub-ideal depths as compensation, with addictions and self-destructive behaviors to follow. We end up becoming a depth-mystery to ourselves again, like when we were infants; addicted persons are trying to return to pre-conscious state out of some strange desire to convert themselves directly into a new depth into which they are perpetually sunken, like a star sinking into a black hole that it itself is forming, and the pain, suffering, unhealth, early death and anger and all the rest that comes with drug addiction is actually preferred by the addict *because such feelings are the form of the development of his self becoming its own depth.* A better depth than drugs, such as love or artistic or philosophic passion, is simply a depth that doesn't require you to turn yourself into a black hole into which to sink and destroy yourself, you can instead get a proper depth-experience without needing to make yourself into that very depth; you can remain somewhat distant

149

from it. Obviously love is the greatest depth, for reasons

Chambers mentions[8].

---

[8] If you want another person to be everything for you, that is possible. But you have to give them everything. And that is almost impossible. But give them everything and they can be everything. Giving them everything means obvious things, like not fucking someone else. But it means other things too. As long as you give them everything, they can be everything, meaning- no matter what happens to you they can save you with a word, even if you're facing death. But giving them everything means risking everything. That risk is difficult … as we are both wounded. But the risk is worth it, because you cannot always save yourself.

In love, we must pour everything that we are into a single feeling, grappling at the margin of our past and future, to transform all the pain we have lived through into it, into love. It is the most dangerous thing a human can do, as we risk what we are, both in having to confront the suffering we buried and now have to dredge up, hold together, organize, and reveal to the other person, and in the possibility of failing this person, in being unable to present this pain in anything other than its bare, crippled nudity; we risk our existence, in love. It is a delicate matter, giving them our pain without drowning them in it, or ourselves. It is the most dangerous thing you can do and it probably is supposed to be. Artistic production is a close second, but even it is far less than that, for, though we can certainly pour a great deal of ourselves into a work of art or a book, we can never give it everything like we can give to love, and we offer a work to the world- a thing always somehow both less and more forgiving than the single individual love offers itself to. I put it this way in one of my books:

"All that takes place at the most remote heights of consciousness, which love certainly does, and, face to face with death, attended by nothing more than the triumphant gaze of the ego at once firmly delivered to its own universe, to its philosophy, takes place without any chance of ever being reabsorbed into the series of causes and effects that produced it, and, unable to return back into the night of the unconscious, or anymore modify the rhythms of our dreams- unable to recapitulate the false univalence of or add itself back to the flat inertia of psychic life, does, in

Another important and useful depth, a more healthy one than

drugs, is holidays such as I was talking about with my comments

---

its conclusive termination, leave behind, unlike the other psychodynamic processes to which we find ourselves subject- which can never find any real fulfillment for themselves or even so much as a conclusion in the world of matter, not a residue, beyond whose epistasis and passive mantle the self-intoxication and impletion of all we ascribe to the name Eros could see beyond, but an empty space, a discontiguity, a rupture from within the libidinal-motive complex itself, in just the same way that it is through music that we escape from time as only from within time, or through prayer and poetry, through the annunciation of an impassioned hallelujah or a declaration of love, that we escape from language by fully penetrating language, leaving it overladen with its own positive contents, with the unconscious, once open merely to exogenous excitations upon the primordial vital impulse around which it accretes anterotically, upon the basis of its reactivity as opposed to activity, thereby rendered palpable to the intellect. It is the first phase in the erotic movement, that all we have said and done before should be swept away into the very dust that our winged angel had turned up in its flight, proving all our life, for all it was, nonetheless but a trifling thing, so that all we have yet to say and to do, though still hold somewhere within ourselves, might be at last performed, and that with the dull superficies of the personality now firmly absumed, our mask finally removed in this- the midnight hour, to speak with Kierkegaard, and the depth of the soul entered into. One cannot lie under the influence of love for, in the depths, all becomes a law, as Rilke says, and the lie can only meet with utterance at that surface whose contours the erotic movement will irretrievably trace, and yet the truth of Eros is not a word, or a deed, but a work- namely, the work which Eros itself, in its second, creative-phase, actually is, whose structure is that of the mythic katabasis- anabasis,- a structure that will slowly engrave itself as Dike or justice upon the structure of Psyche, of the depth of the soul, of the unconscious, with the song of love such a song as might one day become the song of our life." (excerpt from *A Glorious Risk*). Joseph Chambers, personal correspondence, October, 2017.

151

about Christmas. And of course religions are also depths into which many people feel compelled to sink themselves.

The depths exist for us to use to stabilize ourselves in existence, which for us means to secure ourselves existentially (socially and psychologically, which means philosophically) and in such a way that maximally mitigates and compensates for those particular forms that the deficiencies in our own individual souls happen to have taken— to do this also in such a way that is lasting enough to span the entire length of our lives. If we can find that ideal perfect depth in which to sink ourselves and then stay there for however long our lives happen to be, until the day we die, then that is "the whole point". That's what "meaning" means, to us humans anyway and probably to all beings anywhere in existence. Thus I am conditioning the three fundamental existential cores, those of truth, power and fantasy, to this new idea of finding the perfect depth-experience (which highest will probably always be love, real love) and sinking ourselves into it in perpetuity (for however long our lives happen to last). This entire process, as both understanding and as practically living this understanding out in and as our very lives, is what psychology actually is and means.

152

2.

Emotions and thoughts are sublimations of survival "instincts"

(energy, excess), basically that animal life has this basic

constitution and setup where it has this inner frenzy and excess of

self that produces the pool of energy needed for a psychology to

form, this psychology gets structured according to natural

selection, and over time the survival imperative that keeps that

psyche in the structure and form it has, instinctually, ends up

being sublimated by getting increasingly subdivided in the

neurology and also in the hormonal systems, becoming so

fragmented that it gets to be too difficult to reconstitute the

original instinctual response in the presence of certain stimuli and

another method needs to be found to ensure survivability. This

other method was first the development of emotions, basically the

reptile brain/limbic system, because this allowed for

compensation for the loss of some of the integrity of the previous

instinctual psychology; later on, even the emotions became too

fragmented and excessive, and another sublimation needed to take

place to compensate for this, with this second sublimation of

course being what we call thought/thinking, the building of a

conscious and rational inner model that can speak to itself and model itself. Perception was the foundation for this second sublimation that led to what we call thinking, because while in the past perception was just used for seeing the immediate environment perception was also able to be turned on itself and turned inward, and in order to do that we needed upgraded memory capacity so that we could mentally perceive more than one clear perception at a time, thus becoming able to compare and contrast them, thus forming the foundation that thought needed to build itself into existence and act as compensation for the fragmentations of instinctive psychology and emotions with respect to survivability. Thought therefore creating the neocortex out of the frontal lobe, because it needed more brain structures to do this whole inner modeling, meta-perceiving thing.

Imagination is therefore just a kind of memory, a very fragmented and sublimated remembering capacity that breaks apart thousands of remembered things and perceives them in juxtaposed ways that we call "imagination" or "predicting the future". Plato was right. Thought is remembrance, sort of.

Now that thought too is fragmenting its excess will lead to another, third sublimation. Or maybe not. We don't have much else in our physiology to co-opt, we already co-opted feelings and proprioception for creating emotions and we already co-opted perception and memory for creating thought. What else is there to co-opt in ourselves, in our organism?

3.

Daemonic tension is actually a deeper tension than simply that in our 'thoughts', and the tensions and differences in thought cannot really activate or reach the level of tension and difference in the daemonic as such, because thought is like a secondary representation of the deeper variances: basically there were, tens of thousands of years ago, certain instinctual patterns or "drives" that allowed us to survive because they successfully adapted our physical bodies, inner sensations/perception, and our environment to each other in such a way that did not lead us dying off; but these early human animals still had a development of what we call reason, in potentia, due to our neocortex, and we also had advantage of dextrous tongues and mouths and vocal chords which could produce a wide variety of digital sounds; the combination of this budding reason, which would first manifest as a kind of enhanced memory capacity I would think, an improved ability to learn and recall things that have been experienced and have been paired with something meaningful, with the complex vocal utterances we could make and with the fact that these utterances could be exactly copied and reproduced by others because they were so digital, allowed us to form the first stirrings of proper language. We would have been labeling things in the environment with this language, but not directly, rather we would be simply pronouncing a given utterance in the presence of a certain stimuli and doing so entirely "unconsciously", such as: one of these early humans walks into a cave and sees a young naked female, he gets an erection, and then a certain vocal utterances comes out of his mouth which represents this total experience he is having. Others will hear this utterance and see the situation to which it is paired, and the most useful utterances will end up catching on and spreading through the group.

When two of these humans fight, each would shout his own utterances, the ones that he has previously paired with encountering dangerous animals in the wild, for when he is hunting. The human who wins will then shout his personal utterances for the fight over and over, and these will be adopted by others who are watching; thus this human who wins the fight will become more of a leader, more feared, and take more control over the direction of the evolution of the tribe's language.

After thousands of years of that sort of thing, we end up with certain human tribes all over the planet who are all speaking to each other in these different digital languages being used to convey immediate associations to meaningful experiences. A resonance or harmony forms intra-tribe because of the shared vocal utterances and because such utterances are very close to the most essential and immediate meanings of the humans in those tribes (food, hunt, danger, sex, safety, etc.). Now, the same advanced neocortex that allowed us to access having a better memory is also going to take this early language and transform it towards something even more complex, as eventually humans will start noticing and remembering not just the utterance phoneme itself but also the sounds and gestures of the person immediately before and after that phoneme, and connecting these all together... so the phoneme, the sound of the specific word, is also being associated to whatever vocal and gestural context it tends to be most used in, and over time this produces grammar. What we think of as grammar, the highly logical if/then either/or sort of relationships between words, must have been extracted at an even higher level from an earlier grammar that was simply about identifying in what ways certain words could be properly used versus improperly (without meaning) used. So the early language was being refined, and important words were being carefully narrowed down with regard to in what ways they could be used properly, and this would have been done in order to maximize the effectiveness of such words. Like in sign languages across the world, gesture and facial expression are also very important to grammar, in fact in sign languages these ARE most of the grammar.

Thus there are at this point early humans with their simple expressive-associative languages slowly refining toward a more delimited grammar structure. Now that words are being narrowed in their meaning and proper usage, new words need to be found to fill the gaps of the shrinking spaces of meaning and excess. Therefore these languages have vocabularies that naturally expand as their grammar also expands.

I wanted to try and fit all this into your analysis of the daemonic... The *meanings* behind these early languages would be what is in a state of abstraction and tension, is that correct? For example, the word for tiger and the word for spear, in these early human tribes there would have existed a daemonic tension between those two "concepts" (meanings) in the minds of these humans, because these entirely different objects/experiences were being forced together in the field prescribed by the language, and because the one object/experience immediately led to recall and awareness of the other. Therefore, the tension becomes able to be activated by simply touching one side of it: the human could see a tiger or see a spear and immediately part of his mind would mobilize the entire daemonic conception in which he uses a spear to kill a tiger. This mobilization or activation of a specific tension primes him cognitively and physiologically to enact the behaviors associated with those conceptions, and this whole priming process is therefore what is referred to as an instinct. An instinct is just a certain more or less codified, crystallized stimulus and response patterns with regard to a certain abstraction, such abstractions being associations or "concepts" for multiple different things/objects that have previously been experienced as meaningful. Because these instincts are neurologically and hormonally based, certain of these kinds of patterns can actually be passed on epigenetically to offspring, so that the tendency to

159

have an instinctual response to certain stimuli can actually be inherited.

Those instinctive patterns that became most critically important for the tribe's survival and flourishing (defeating its enemies, i.e. other human tribes) would have been solidified in the neurology and physiology of the bodies of the humans in those tribes, and it is these that I am thinking of as proper drives. Would this be close to your own usage of the term 'drive'? Very stabilized and crystallized instinctive patterns, with instinctive patterns as defined as above, namely associations between multiple different things that produce a delimited range of stimuli and response behaviors. So these drives develop and become constitutive of the social fabric of the tribe, there are drives for hunting, sex, family, social status, hiding, shelter, making clothes, making fire, etc. These drives are therefore like *very deep concepts*, or very central ideas for the tribe. But even now, at this point the humans in these tribes are not really thinking, are not really self-aware or self-conscious. The development of a self, that must come later when there can be a way of separating out the individual person from this total drive-conscious immersion which is the social fabric of ideas and assocations. So this occurred at the end of the many

160

pagan tribal evolutions which produced hosts of different and complex and competing drive-arrangements, societies, namely in Ancient Greece these pagan systems were able to be adapted in the light of reason, as thinking became something finally individual, critical, and separate from the extant social fabric.

The Greeks inherited a vast pagan tradition of so many and such complex drive systems that, based on the world of a small number of highly intelligent men, the pre-Socratics, were able to separate out from these to a certain degree and apply words in a new way, to compare and contrast the words directly with themselves and entirely in their minds... they could wonder like Thales about the nature of the elements and if water is more essential than fire, for example. This sort of usage of language was entirely new, and it side-stepped the traditional symbols and mythic systems in which the words/utterances had previously always been organized; such symbols and myths being the gods, for example. The pre-Socratics invented a new way of using language, they started using words to directly compete and contrast and compare with other words, to push concepts together in their minds and to find a way of testing the result, to see which concept was superior (could include the other). This sort of thing is what allowed language to develop a

161

proper grammar, or at least allowed proper logic to form. There must have been a parallel evolution of this same process that occurred in the ancient Greek world also having had occurred in the ancient Egyptian/Judaic world, since the Jews have their own alphabetical system and grammar logic, but I am not well versed in the history of languages to know much about that (you probably know a lot about it). Anyway, so there are many parallel evolutions of this kind going on around the world, where a small number of intelligent people in a tribe are learning how to use language to "think about" what that language is saying/expressing. Eventually philosophies are born, and more complex religious are born, and conceptual abstract thinking for its own sake become possible. It would be at this point where "the self" could finally appear, because the self is simply the remainder in the thinking process, it is whatever is not being thought about at any given moment... when we think something, the content of that thought is what we focus on, and we derive our existence as a self from the fact that "we" are the ones "doing the thinking", which literally means that whatever is not being thought about in that moment is acting as the implicit basis and foundation from which what is being thought is being thought. Like carving out a space in rock for a river to wind through, the water is the content of the thoughts, the rock bed is the self. This is how the "river" would experience itself, it has this "self" that does not change (the rock bed) and then it has these "thoughts" or mental impressions (the water) that moves through that unchanging thing.

So the experience of having a self is a creation of this kind of abstract rational thinking capacity and of the kind of language that makes it possible... maybe. Of course it is way more complex than that. I only wanted to develop this basic level of analysis here so I could get to the point of seeing what the daemonic tensions are:

Thoughts (final development of a "self" (of ability to compare/contrast the drives as such, in the mind only)

Drives (human social, level higher organization of the most essential instincts)

Instincts (animal level)

Basic linguistic utterances (all animals have basic communication)

That (above) is how I am thinking about it, from top to bottom following the arrows. So there would be daemonic tensions at all levels of this, and the resonance of one tension could lead to others at other levels since the structure is harmonized not only horizontally but also vertically.

The Greek method of thinking led to Christianity, which is as Chambers says a reinterpretation of the excess as a lack and employing a single image-symbol, God, as a stand-in for this lack. This is fascinating because Christians took the significant excess of conceptions and their underlying drives that had been built up before it and, rather than philosophizing about it and making art and politics in terms of it as the old Greeks did, instead unified this excess into a single feeling, one "depth-experience" with one name, "God", and the associated feeling to this name was one of lack. Christianity probably did all this because it couldn't understand the excess. Then God becomes the symbol of the lack, to which humans can relate themselves and "fill in" that lack somehow.

4.

Irreconcilability of the Tensions:

164

Not only are the elements of one tension, namely its polarities, irreducible to each other but also it is the case that two or more tensions entered into relation with each other are also irreducible to one another as that very relation, and indeed this is what it means for tensions to enter into relation with each other: that they become irreducible and unable to produce a 'reconciliation' beyond this shared dynamic of relation from which ushers forth a derivative tension greater in power and higher up within the continuum of being than are those individual tensions which comprise that dynamic itself. The world cannot be reduced to any one individual mind unless that mind already includes all of the tensions that in their dynamic relations with each inform the groundwork and motivating structure of the world, and this is why most people are unable to comprehend the world just as it is also the reason why the pursuit of knowledge leads necessarily into suffering and self-negation, into what is sometimes called evil: only by seeking into every conceivable tension and relation of tensions, whether deemed Good or Bad, whether painful or pleasurable, right or wrong, etc. can we approach a sufficiently comprehensive model of all tensions that exist in this reality, for example in this world and society or also in this psyche and self, if

165

it is our goal to understand these. And it is also the case that the suffering and evil caused by the unrepentant search for knowledge is only redeemable in this higher threshold of understanding, to which the knowledge of suffering and evil, if not those sufferings and evils themselves, becomes a necessity. Without this greater tectonic of knowledge that aims for sufficiency with regard to the accuracy and completeness of that which it aims to model in its understanding, knowledge itself becomes only one more destabilizing force within the existing dynamics of the tensions, for we are unable to raise the discordant harmony of the tensions any higher with the introduction of this knowledge, namely with the introduction of new tensions and of new ways of relating the tensions to each other, which is what knowledge always is and always presupposes.

Another insight connected to this: "meaning" is basically a pure excess, the fact that a reaction engendered in us by something is greater than is actually necessary to that thing which caused the reaction. This is "irrational" only at a basis level, at higher levels it actually primes us to become sensitive to facts (aspects of reality) that we otherwise would not have known because did not need to know. It also develops the psyche directly, it also makes life more potent and causal-motivating for us, and it also eventually creates the meaning that it at first simply "faked" by having that initial over-reaction.

Then later on we narrow down this excessive range of meaning, making it less excessive and more sufficient to the actually-necessary; this process of narrowing it down is also what philosophy is. But it cannot ever be narrowed down so far as to become coextensive with the necessary, because that would destroy the excess, therefore a kind of back and forth dance and dynamic balancing occurs of philosophy trying to approximate necessity as such as much as possible and the meaning-psychological excess pushing back against that as much as possible. Neither side can "win", this is just another daemonic tension.

5.

What we call right and left in politics are actually two limits, one upper limit and one lower limit, to a certain substance in the middle of these limits, which substance we might call human being in a social-political sense, or perhaps we may call it the human world. The upper limit is characterized by the limits of thinking, while the lower limit is characterized by the limits of feeling; right and left will switch places as to which takes on the role of representing either limit, for example currently the right is representing the upper limit of thought when it comes to much of modern politics such as issues of immigration and national sovereignty, because these issues and the crises surrounding them represent limits of our ability to think about such things more than do they represent limits of feeling, and in fact we can observe how the limit of feeling, the lower limit, is in the case of these examples acting as a kind of gravity that pulls people down from thought and keeps them further bound to the thought-limit. This is precisely how these two limits work, as a daemonic tension: the substance in the middle, which can be characterized as human being, mind, life, or world, is pulled toward both limits because on the other side of each limit is a significant reality that is presently inaccessible to us, but the limit itself acts as both the focal point of the draw of this excess reality as well as the barrier through which we cannot break and thus prevents us from accessing that excess reality, so that the limit achieves the dual function of symbolizing the excess and of preventing our access to the excess. Because there is always a much more significant scope of reality in thought

168

as well as in feeling than we are able to access, the limits of thought and feeling both act in this dual manner of pulling us toward them while simultaneously also pushing us away, and then these two limits work together on both sides of the middle substance in order to delimit this middle space, which is what "humanity" and "the world" is, and this middle space is both drawn toward the upper and lower limits of itself as well as repelled by those same limits. Numerous tensions proliferate between the two limits, with each such tension being another specific issue in politics, psychology, ethics, etc., and indeed these fields which are often called "social sciences" and to the degree they are not scientific in the true sense, do constitute the outward image and representation of daemonic tensions within the substance, and most of these daemonic tensions exist between the upper and lower limits of the substance.

The political right and left will take turns as to which represents the upper or lower limit at any given time and with regard to any given issue, as these change over time, but due to the proliferation of daemonic tensions within the substance and between these two limits, as soon as either right or left switches and takes on a certain role with respect to a limit, it becomes the case that the other must take the opposing role. Indeed, the right will also take on the role of representing the lower limit of feeling, and the left will also take on the role of representing the upper limit of thought, when it comes to certain issues and at certain moments in time/history. This is why progress in a political and social sense is so slow and fraught with chaos, why it is so irrational in its process—in order to expand the substance, which is what "progress in a political and social sense" means, both left and right need to reorient their polarities and alliances to some degree, because it is not the case that right or left are tied only to one of the limits but are in fact bound up to both limits in complex and often irrational ways. Thus right and left in the political sense do not truly exist except as phantoms, as a kind of false symbolization of unique combinations of daemonic tensions that otherwise would not combine like that, and neither left or right owns either the limit of thought or the limit of feeling, although as I mentioned at certain times it will appear as if right or left does represent one of these limits much more strongly than the other. Right and left are more like incidental arrangements of combinations of certain tensions with regard to the two limits, and right and left over time tend to draw into their nexus or push away from their nexus certain tensions according to a structural logic which requires the left and right to maintain their coherence and structural-logical integrity first and only to maintain actual logical and rational consistency second. Only the two limits exist, and the middle substance, only these have actual real existence, while left and right only exist as partial reflections and symbols of certain arrangements and combinations of different parts of that substance-in-development and with regard to the limits of thought and of feeling.

I was thinking about the politics of left and right, and realized that left and right do not actually exist...

What we call right and left in politics are actually two limits, one upper limit and one lower limit, to a certain substance in the middle of these limits, which substance we might call human being in a social-political sense, or perhaps we may call it the human world. The upper limit is characterized by the limits of thinking, while the lower limit is characterized by the limits of feeling; right and left will switch places as to which takes on the role of representing either limit, for example currently the right is actively representing more so the upper limit of thought when it comes to much of modern politics (but is then also passively representing the lower limit of feeling on precisely the same issues) such as issues of immigration and national sovereignty, because these issues and the crises surrounding them represent limits of our ability to think about such things more than do they represent limits of feeling, and in fact we can observe how the limit of feeling, the lower limit, is in the case of these examples acting as a kind of gravity that pulls people down from thought and keeps them further bound to the thought-limit. This is precisely how these two limits work, as a daemonic tension: the substance in the middle, which can be characterized as human being, mind, life, or world, is pulled toward both limits because on the other side of each limit is a significant reality that is presently inaccessible to us, but the limit itself acts as both the focal point of the draw of this excess reality as well as the barrier through which we cannot break and thus prevents us from accessing that excess reality, so that the limit achieves the dual function of symbolizing the excess and of preventing our access to the excess. Because there is always a much more significant scope of reality in thought as well as in feeling than we are able to access, the limits of thought and feeling both act in this dual manner of pulling us toward them while simultaneously also pushing us away, and then these two limits work together on both sides of the middle

172

substance in order to delimit this middle space, which is what "humanity" and "the world" is, and this middle space is both drawn toward the upper and lower limits of itself as well as repelled by those same limits. Numerous tensions proliferate between the two limits, with each such tension being another specific issue in politics, psychology, ethics, etc., and indeed these fields which are often called "social sciences" and to the degree they are not scientific in the true sense, do constitute the outward image and representation of daemonic tensions within the substance, and most of these daemonic tensions exist between the upper and lower limits of the substance.

The political right and left will take turns as to which represents the upper or lower limit at any given time and with regard to any given issue, as these change over time, but due to the proliferation of daemonic tensions within the substance and between these two limits, as soon as either right or left switches and takes on a certain role with respect to a limit, it becomes the case that the other must take the opposing role. Indeed, the right will also take on the role of representing the lower limit of feeling, and the left will also take on the role of representing the upper limit of thought, when it comes to certain issues and at certain moments in time/history. This is why progress in a political and social sense is so slow and fraught with chaos, why it is so irrational in its process—in order to expand the substance, which is what "progress in a political and social sense" means, both left and right need to reorient their polarities and alliances to some degree, because it is not the case that right or left are tied only to one of the limits but are in fact bound up to both limits in complex and often irrational ways. Thus right and left in the political sense do not truly exist except as phantoms, as a kind of false symbolization of unique combinations of daemonic tensions that otherwise would not combine like that, and neither left or right owns either the limit of thought or the limit of feeling, although as I mentioned at certain times it will appear as if right or left does represent one of these limits much more strongly than the other. Right and left are more like incidental arrangements of combinations of certain tensions with regard to the two limits, and right and left over time tend to draw into their nexus or push away from their nexus certain tensions according to a structural logic which requires the left and right to maintain their coherence and structural-logical integrity first and only to maintain actual logical and rational consistency second. **Only the two limits exist and the middle substance have actual real existence, while left and**

right only exist as 'metaphysical' partial reflections and symbols of certain arrangements and combinations of different parts of that substance-in-development and with regard to the limits of thought and of feeling. "Left and right politics and political ideology" does not actually exist, not really.

With politics, a main problem is that left and right care more about their structural consistency in the moment than they do about historical or logical consistency. This is somewhat necesssry since left and right are really just averages of daemonic processes all thrust together into a nexus and what we call left or right is just the result and outward expression of those underground tectonics, as a true averaging toward the middle of the nexus, but the problem with this is obviously that left and right end up taking on these absurd positions and forms because left and right are not even conscious things, they are unconscious. The right has now moved toward secularism even as if retains mostly Christian elements and has moved toward libertarian anti-war small government even though neocons still exist in plenty in many of the right parties in the west, so basically the pro big government pro war and pro religious aspect of "the right" is all collapsing or fragmenting right now, while of course the left has abandoned its own secularism for Islam and has embraced big government and war and censorship all of which used to be largely on the right.

But these changes don't really mean anything for right and left themselves, since right and left don't actually mean anything other than an averaging toward the center of those two nexuses within the daemonic tectonics of the life/Mind/world substance of the human being. Traditional positive functions of the left are breaking down as it turns toward totalitarianism and deliberate ignorance as values, but these are no more fundamental aspects of the left than they are of the right also, namely those values aren't fundamental to either left or right but just appear in predominance at certain times and places based on how the underlying daemonic tensions are being averaged there. And then right and left both average around each other because they must avoid any significant overlap, which means they force each other into weird positions. We have two halves of our bodies and our brains, we also have two halves of our social political sphere, left and right so called, and also there are two "halves" of the underlying human substance namely the two limits I mentioned, of thinking and of

176

feeling, but right and left just dance around with those limits and neve really align fully with one of the other. So two limits that are fixed but expand over time as the substance expands, and then two social political limits of left and right which aren't limits so much as purely averaging tendencies that can only approximate the limits and the tensions.

And there must be a massive storm in the daemonics right now to have Trump get elected. Trump is like s lightning rod signifier that is forcing and allowing totally new averagings to occur. Thus the limits are probably about to be pushed back once again.

I think that some people have hearts too sensitive for the rest of life beyond their dreams; the world and other people are far more crude and painful than are our images of these things when we are young, so the hope you mention becomes damaged and must either be protected or abandoned. Philosophers abandon it, for truth, while poets and romantics protect it with their very lives, because it is so valuable to them. Loosely this corresponds to male and female psyches, respectively. "Less and more emotional", and conversely "more and less rational".

What is weird about myself is that I have both of these psyches, both natures are overpowering in me and neither can ever give way to the other. I don't vacillate between dreams and truth, I contain both at all times, maximally. To me, love means to nurture these natures in another and to the degree either nature or psyche is fundamental and important to the other person, even taking on the burden of immense guilt for it. I dislike guilt of course, but I force it into a forge within my ideas and feelings and it becomes transformed over time into a higher threshold of "balance" between those two psyches. My passions for hope and for truth, for dreams and for the world, for "emotions" and "reasons" are both solidified and elevated over time, I think, as guilt enlarges my soul.

Almost nothing is as destabilizing of consciousness as is really deep guilt, I hate it, but it forces me to increase and grow around that wound, and to learn from it so that I can value better next time, make less mistakes and be a bit more conscious the next time around. And then any remnants of guilt that linger are motivations to plunge back into love, hope, joy again.

The dynamics and development of guilt and romantic love afforded by Christianity are indeed very profound. Your analyses of liberal secular humanism as abandonment of this is very pertinent and accurate I would say. But liberal secular humanism is also in small amounts (in youth, for example) only an excess that actually causes further increase in "Christian-like valuing" and this guilt-love psychological method by acting in opposition to it, forcing delimitations that trigger more growth, like pruning a tree. All of these methods whether Christian or liberal secular humanist are not meant to become a totalizing ethos or personality type, they are meant to act like bridges that we eventually cross when we have built up enough of the substance which the methods afford our souls. These diehard fundamentalist religious or SJW types are simply people who have mistaken a method for a personality, mistaken the form for the substance, like Analytic philosophy does. Such people were always simply not deep enough in contact with their own substance for whatever reason and unable to distinguish on an "instinctive" level between those methods and those more true, unspeakable substances which they really are.

In its more benign form, liberal secular humanism in its psychological aspect is a limit on Christian valuing-method that helps keep us from being absorbed unduly into that method, keeps us from mistaking that method for our very souls. So there is a daemonic tension between Christianity and Liberal Secular Humanism, which daemonic is being worked out presently in and as the western world right now.

At bottom, the desire to know is destructive of the desire to be; equally it is the case that knowledge itself is, in extremity, non-being itself, or death, for to know one must rip such knowledge from oneself to hold it up isolated and separate from oneself, a different thing entirely, not dead but neither living as it once was, and then in the best case to trap this broken and torn thing, this knowledge, into the forms of language as I am presently doing with this very thought, with this very... knowledge that I am writing to you. True knowledge is structured and dimensional being, and its geometry sits in the soul as part of a patchwork. To tear out this knowledge we gain familiarity with its shape and geometry, but what is lost is the intimate familiarity with which such pieces of ourselves fit so perfectly in place, this familiarity being the very soul itself as the soul's own excess that cannot be

180

touched but may only touch, that cannot endure form and the light of day save through many transformations and veils, many intermediary stages which are needed to buffer the soul's depths from the hell of life, from the world which is a construct of being that could never become being itself.

Such a tectonic height of understanding as is capable of perceiving this fact, as is capable of knowing without destroying and of in knowledge loving without perverting, would in a practical sense be required to move through much of its own opposite, namely that destruction and perversion, and would for this reason be almost impossible to obtain—indeed would be impossible if not for the very excess of its own process, which communicates a little bit of destruction in every achievement of knowing and, where knowing aims to love, a little bit of subversion and fantasy in every achievement of reality in and through love. Love makes itself known but is not knowledge itself. Love is far less knowledge than being, for every striving of spirit toward reality must take place upon a foundation of the soul's own excess if it is not to subvert its own purpose and aim, if it is not to degenerate into a mere species of... worldly things, secondary things, things that are constructed but do not construct.

The excess is deep at the bottom of the soul, and only the soul is deep enough to contain it; to reach the arm of knowledge down to these depths and grasp being itself, pulling it up into the light—not of day, but of a kind of pale vision whose very transience spurs on the endlessly unsatisfied effort of itself—this has been an unconscious aim of mankind and has ultimately given us religions, sciences and politics, the mutual fusion of which promises to finally achieve our dream of "immortality", by which of course is meant that no longer will man suffer his own excess, no longer will he merely be without knowing... no longer will the soul rule over the mind, over "consciousness". This obsessive project has no contrary and no match anywhere else, no pole in opposition to itself save for the very soul-depth and excess, true substance of being, that it aims to overcome.

Each work gets shorter as work progresses, a benefit of time that is also a loss of time and which further isolates us from others in whom such work does not take shape, in whom the restless spirit reflects only the secondary world and in whom never does the soul find more possibility to life than where it has already been suppressed behind merely created things—and even this is still such a soul's hope, to live best as a shadow of life itself and in such humility to give to life at least something truly of life itself, so that the world may endure its own burdensome weight for another moment and even if such an endurance rarely extends beyond such a simple sufficiency. Yet while being contented in many cases with such a function this is not the soul's own substance, and thus could only ever express a small hope and never a truly great one: it is rather the greatest hope of the soul to achieve equality with the world where it comes to reconciling knowledge to being which balance and reconciliation is known by another word, namely love, while in this phenomenon of love resides the secret of the creation of time itself, with finally the co-expression of love and time constituting the core of the experience of joy, the most fundamentally human experience on which all other human experiences rest and depend. Joy, which is the creating co-expression of love and time through knowledge's reconciliation to being, is the very basis of all desiring and structures all motivational human acts, and therefore it is also the case that joy may most be abused, ignored or taken for granted and still manage to give something of itself adequate for the maintenance of a life, although in such cases never more than this bare sufficiency. It is therefore joy's hope to raise itself beyond sufficiency, that it might share in the soul's own excess and lead to the transformation of life in the image of joyful being.

6.

Man's capacity for brutality and violence is matched only by his capacity for gentleness and kindness, and both of these capacities, being each unlimited to itself save by the exhaustion of its psychological application which mere entropy could never serve as a proper and hard, true limit, can only be properly limited by the other; our gentle nature limits our violent nature just as our violent nature limits our gentle nature, and each must be strong enough to fortify the other, as hard resistance, as a true limit. This is not to prevent either capacity for maximizing itself in some asymptotic climb to the absolute expression, because again the psychological entropic reality prevents this, but is rather to prevent them from acceding entirely to this entropy and thereby exhausting themselves entirely. The merely psychological limit is not an "upper" limit but rather is a "lower" limit, and the only way to conceive an upper limit, which is to say to set a proper delimitation from the perspective of truth, is to educate these two natures. Such an education can only occur when the mere fact of duality is turned into a dynamic mutual relation—into a daemonic tension. Each of these two natures must be made to become part of a larger nature that both derives from as well as transforms the original two. This third nature, made out of the active delimiting conflict and irreconcilable difference between the original two natures, is simply what we call human nature. Human nature is not just the sum of our contrasting capacities for violence and kindness, however we would like to define those two natures, but is an entirely new sort of nature made not only from a blending of those two but becomes in fact something entirely new, for each of those two original natures is radically transformed and becomes something entirely new in their mutual combination with and limitation by one another, and especially in so far as the third nature grows into something not only limiting and combinatory of those two, but in fact attains to its own true nature and scope in both a psychological as well as philosophical meaning.

Each of the original two natures is made to individualize itself more and more by being thrust together in mutual delimitation under the new third term or third nature, and this process and priority of individuality is on par with the same process and prioritization of individuality as occurs in the world of nature, as what we call natural selection—individual creatures acting by their own self-value prioritize themselves and enter into daemonic relationships with each other, achieving mutual limitation and an increased need for individuality in doing so, and the nature of this relationality expresses itself as conflict, which conflict becomes a new "third term" in which substance those same individuals participate both directly and indirectly: directly by forging that substance into proper being as what we call society, and indirectly by being themselves forged by that substance and according to its rules, norms, and needs. The daemonic relationship between individual and society mirrors the daemonic relationship between our gentle and our violent natures, and although there is no immediate 1:1 correspondence between both daemonisms, since each is qualitatively different from the other, a correspondence relation does develop between them and constitutes a new, larger daemonism of "mankind itself", with this new relation and daemonic substance coming into existence by virtue of what we call religion. Religion or metaphysical-mythological substance is the means by which the two primary daemonic tensions (that of our violent and gentle natures on the one hand and of the individual and society on the other hand) are brought together in the following way: the concepts of Good and Bad are created at

186

the beginning of language's development, far back in human pre-history, and these concepts serve as mechanisms by which our violent and gentle natures can be related to one another through the medium of society. Religion is less about creating an initial ontology and more about creating an initial ethics, whereby the application of this ethics requires the mutual appearance of a basic epistemological framework and which epistemological framework in turn requires the existence of some degree of ontological assumptions. Religion speaks to "what is" only in so far as is needed for it to be able to speak to "what is our knowing", and it speaks to "what is our knowing" only in so far as is needed for it to be able to speak to "what must we do". We must know what we must do, in order to do it, and we must have some schema of reality in order to ground what we must know. This is the order of priorities in religious constructs, and at basic these constructs serve to allow the two primary daemonisms (of our dual individual natures and of the duality of individual and society) to relate to each other through the basic ethical impulse which expresses itself as the universality and psychological undeniability of the two categories of Good and Bad, or right and wrong. In this way the substance 'individual plus society' is able to regulate consistent expressions of both of individual man's natures,

187

destructive and civilizing, as needed to form over time the sort of equations and patterns of application and limitation of each that prove to be required for society (and "the human species") to continue to exist and advance itself, which advancement and existence hinges upon the same kind of naturally selective experimentation that gives rise to the natural world and all of life. The only difference is that man expresses and experiences thus naturally selective logical impetus indirectly and his consciously applied reason, as his own individuality and the self-valuing prioritization of himself as "subjectivity", whereas the other creatures of nature express and experience the same naturally selective logical mandate directly, as a severe limitation by which logic they are absolutely bound. Mankind can overcome natural selection but only because it has, in our individuality and sociality, replicated at a higher level the basic logic that is underneath natural selection.

Notes: Daemonic tensions to further analyze:

1. Communism vs. capitalism ("left vs. right") –Postmodernism is part of the formation of the early conditions of a 1984-style world, which is already well under way of forming. The denigration of the category of the individual as sacrosanct, the elevation of an automatic respect for actions of State power so long as these serve an end that one already desires (or has been led to believe they desire) including the constant attempts to disarm the western populace and make them absolutely dependent upon the State for their security and protection by removing their ability, in potentiality and in actuality, for defending themselves (and this also includes the deep psychological impact of knowing that you cannot reasonably defend either yourself or your loved ones, which psychological effect is another part of the underlying forces driving humanity toward an all-encompassing embrace of the State), and how argumentation and discussion, in particular around social and political issues or any issues that are able to be framed in those contexts, are becoming more and more based on feelings and half-hidden signals of allegiance, rather than on an attempt at objective and rational, fact-finding discourse. News media has changed from at least on the surface an attempt at

objective rational fact-finding to an overt appeal to feelings and the half-hidden gestures of solidarity and signals of allegiance to the 'proper' politically correct doctrines and attitudes of the moment; all of these phenomena are signs that we not only approach the 1984-style world but that we are already there. The fact that Trump won is a situation of the exception proving the rule, and of how the elements of sanity will react when provoked too far and pressured into a corner. But if the fact that the more sane elements of western humanity are only able to act in concert, against the postmodern-Marxist-1984 slide that we are trapped in, when provoked so intensely and when pressured into a corner with their backs against the wall, then it is the case that these sane elements have already admitted defeat, for their psychological energy, their motivation, their will-power, and their capacity to act are no longer their own but have become merely a secondary thing, requiring certain conditions from the external environment in order to come to life.

The political and social Left is dead, those such as Zizek, Chomsky and Sam Harris are its death pangs and the bubbles of blood that rise from its throat as it struggles for one final breath. Real leftism has been co-opted by neoliberalism and by the power of mere images and feeling, so that the dutiful leftist mob has become a true mob in the fullest meaning, a Marxist frenzy of 'social justice' taking place in the total absence of anything remotely resembling rational or sane interpersonal discourse or self-reflection. The days of those such as Deleuze and Guattari are all but gone, although it is not without irony that Deleuze and Guattari and others like them laid more of the groundwork for the transformation of the genuine left into the neoliberal, irrational mob-like, 1984-style monster we see before us today, just as Hardt and Negri are hard at work at the present time trying to adapt something resembling (can be sold as) philosophy to the new landscape of State power in all its forms both subtle and not so subtle. An entire industry has arisen around the work of justifying State power and of making the automatic allegiance to State power feel good. This work also includes the use of intellectual jargon and style in an attempt to further force the rational, thinking mind to gloss over any contradictions or problems that might arise in the course of consuming the products of this industry; an industry of propaganda, yes certainly, but it goes much further than that. It is more like an industry of the production of feelings and of personalities in line with a particular ethos, or rather with a particular lack of ethos.

2. Religion vs. atheism

3. Feminism vs. femininity, in terms of self-ownership

4. Power (will to power) vs. love (the proper depth-experience of real love)

5. Technology as a necessity for artistic self-creation vs. technology as the death of artistic creation

www.ingramcontent.com/pod-product-compliance
Lightning Source LLC
Chambersburg PA
CBHW060502290526
45791CB00001B/237